ONCE

From Jap.   .ka
By Amphib.   . Jeep!

Boyé Lafayette De Mente

***

Phoenix Books / Publishers
ISBN: 0-914778-04-8

Other Books by the Author

Japanese Etiquette & Ethics in Business
Korean Business Etiquette
Korean in Plain English
Japanese in Plain English
Chinese Etiquette & Ethics in Business
Businessman's Guide to Japan
Survival Japanese / Instant Japanese
Japan Made Easy—All You Need to Know
to Enjoy Japan
Diner's Guide to Japan
Shopper's Guide to Japan
Etiquette Guide to Japan
Japan's Cultural Code Words
Chinese in Plain English
China's Cultural Code Words
Mexican Cultural Code Words
Mexican Etiquette & Ethics:
Anticipating & Understanding
Mexican Social & Business Behavior
Korea's Business & Cultural Code Words
There is a Word for it in Mexico
KATA—The Key to Understanding & Dealing
With the Japanese
Asian Face Reading
The Japanese Samurai Code: Classic Strategies Success
Samurai Strategies—43 Keys to Success from Musashi
Miyamoto's Classic "Book of Five Rings"
Cultural Code Words of the Hopi People
Cultural Code Words of the Navajo People
Instant Chinese / Survival Chinese
Instant Korean / Survival Korean

Acknowledgement

Without the very generous help and hospitality of several hundred people whom we met along the way, the journey by amphibious jeep from Japan to Alaska would have been many times more difficult, much more hazardous, and might have ended in failure, if not disaster.

I therefore gratefully dedicate this account of the adventure to James Lowell, John Rohrbough, Thomas Winn, and those unnamed and unknown who contributed so much to its success.

Boyé Lafayette De Mente
Tokyo, 1964

Prologue No. 1

On May 3, 1957, Boyé Lafayette De Mente, then a 28-year-old American journalist living in Japan, left Tokyo aboard a 5' 7" x 17' amphibious jeep called *Half-Safe*, with Ben Carlin, an Australian. Four months later to the day the two adventurers arrived in Anchorage, Alaska, ending one of the most remarkable and best-publicized crossings ever made of the Pacific Ocean.

This is De Mente's account of the voyage. (The circumnavigation of the globe by *Half-Safe,* including the North Pacific and Bering Sea crossing, is listed in the *Guinness Book of World Records*, in the Road Vehicles category.)

Note from the Author

December 1987
Tokyo, Japan

More than 30 years have passed since my voyage on Half-Safe, on which I was both crewman and passenger, yet the experience is still fresh in my memory. A series of events that began in 1974 prompted the re-publication of my version of the crossing of the Pacific in Half-Safe (my partner's account was written years ago, but as far as I know is still unpublished.)

This new limited (1987) edition was published primarily for those people whose lives touched mine during the course of the voyage, and who for various reasons, did not obtain a copy of the original edition.

I am reproducing here some of the recent letters and news clippings inspired by ongoing interest in the voyage. The following is excerpted from the February 12, 1974 issue of the *Daily News*, Perth, Australia, and was written by Kirwan Ward, a columnist for the paper (it was sent to me by John Rohrbough, whom I met on Shemya Island in the Aleutian chain in 1957, our first landfall after leaving Japan):

Perth, WA, Tuesday,
February 12, 1974

BEN CARLIN? That's right, he's the bloke who went round the world—water and all, storms, tides, mountains, monsoons, deserts, jungles and all in an amphibious jeep. He is, to understate it, an uncommon man, nagged by the strange compulsion that motivates all such men to do things the hard way.

Compared with the Carlin way, of one man against all the crushing forces of nature and economics, those Skylab characters had an armchair ride. In a craft never designed for crossing large bodies of water, he sailed 9600 miles, occasionally hindered, but never beaten, by wind and wave, by bandit and bureaucrat.

When Carlin first dreamed the impossible dream there wasn't one person who didn't try to talk him out of it. Even the manufacturers of the jeep, when he approached them, told him he was mad and almost shooed him off the premises . But he did it and if you haven't read his book, *Half-Safe*, you should do so at the first opportunity. It is a staggering story of the sea, of navigation, and of the stubborn guts of a man determined to do his own thing no matter what.

Now Ben Carlin is home again in Perth, looking, he says, for "a small job" because, after seeing the world as few humans see it, he is convinced that Perth is the best place in the English-speaking world for a man to live. As for people "when I lived in Kalgoorlie I knew the finest blokes I've ever met anywhere in my life."

Carlin's historic jeep, surely as strange a craft as ever sailed any sea—and I'm not forgetting *Kon Tiki*—is now in Baltimore, Maryland, U.S.A., in good condition.

He told me: "I could drive her now from Perth to Sydney without any trouble at all."

Last year Carlin unsuccessfully offered his jeep to the WA Museum, for the Fremantle Maritime Museum seemed to him— as it does to me—to be the fitting resting place for a craft historically unique in the world and a reminder of a great West Australian adventure . Even if it means pushing out a 1928 motor car to make room for it.

#

Note from the Author

Requests for copies of *Once A Fool* continued to pick up. In 1982 I contacted Thomas J. Winn, who had been the Northwest Airlines Station Manager on Shemya Island when Carlin and I arrived there aboard Half-Safe in the early summer of 1957, to borrow some of the photographs he had taken of the jeep during our stopover. [My own photographs were destroyed in a fire in Tokyo years earlier.]

Tom's reply:
Dear Boye:
I have enclosed 26 color slides and 10 BW negatives of the Shemya adventure as per your request. Please return when no longer required. I have not located a negative of the photograph displayed on the cover of your book, *Once A Fool,* but will keep searching and enquiring of others who were on the scene at that time.

I have read the book and found it intensely interesting, especially for one who was there and could relive the entire affair. The title fits the story and I imagine you will never again risk your life on such a ridiculous voyage.

I have called Bill Johnson and advised him that a special book, autographed by Boyé De Mente, is here for his pleasure. I will call Mr. McHenry this week and tell him about our visit to you and will also ask for photographs he may have of the SYA trip.

Now if you don't mind, I would like about a dozen of your business cards for distribution to NWA personnel and others who have an interest in your books, especially about Japan. One of my friends lived in Tokyo for about nine years and married a Japanese girl. They now live here in MSP. He speaks the language.

All for now, Boyé and as the Irish say, "May the wind always be at your back."

Regards, Tom Winn

###

The following excerpt is from the January 1986 issue of CAR and DRIVER. It appeared in a section called *The Ten Best Amazing Stories*, written by John Hilton:

Half-Safe

If Australian engineer Ben Carlin had done something more risky in World War II than build latrines, he probably would never have developed a compulsion to circle the world in an amphibious jeep. But he didn't, and he did.

By Carlin's own account, the amphibious jeep was among the least successful of the war's inspired improvisations. Unlike its larger cousin, the DUKW amphibious truck, the small jeep could be swamped by the slightest chop. "Its military uses were pretty well confined to light amphibious reconnaissance, ferrying high-powered generals, and serving as bait for nurses and Red Cross girls," Carlin wrote in his 1955 book, Half-Safe.

"Half-Safe" is the name Carlin gave the Ford-made amphibian he bought at a surplus auction. Financed chiefly by back pay from the Royal Engineers, Carlin bolted on a water-tight superstructure, coated the vessel with neoprene, and added numerous fuel tanks.

Then, in August 1948, he and his American-born wife, Elinore (who was prone to seasickness), set sail from New York.

The New York departure was just for show: *Life* magazine, which had chipped in $500, insisted on it. Carlin actually set out from Montreal via Halifax, Nova Scotia.

Weather and mechanical problems aborted four attempts at crossing the Atlantic. The Carlins finally got as far as the Azores—sometimes hoisting sail to increase the jeep's three-knot pace—in the summer of 1950.

From the Azores the Carlins island-hopped to northern Africa, and thence to Europe. After crossing the Straits of Gibraltar, they were arrested for an unauthorized landfall at an RAF base. By the time they reached Paris, they were so broke they exhibited "Half-Safe" in department stores to raise funds.

Carlin spent three years in England refitting his vehicle and writing his book, while Elinore supported them as a typist for the U.S. Air Force.

"From Paris our proper route lies overland to Calcutta via Istanbul, Damascus, Bagdad, Teheran, Kabul and Delhi," he wrote at the end of Half-Safe. Then "by water to Rangoon; overland to Saigon via Bangkok; by sea and land to Alaska via the Philippines, Formosa, Okinawa, Japan and the Aleutians, and finally by land to Montreal and New York via anywhere."

Just how the rest of the trip went is something of a mystery. That it was completed we know from a terse six-paragraph item in the *New York Times* of June 2, 1958. Headed "Seagoing Jeep Ends World Tour," it noted Carlin's return to New York.

But the *Times* never really understood the point of the whole thing. It noted that only 9500 miles of the roughly 50,000-mile junket had been covered at sea—and then indexed the account under "Ocean Voyages."

The *Guinness Book of World Records* provides a few more clues to what may be the least documented of modern automotive adventures. Crediting Carlin with "the only circumnavigation of the world by an amphibious vehicle," the editors add that "he was accompanied on the trans-Atlantic stage by his ex-wife Elinore (US) and on the long transpacific stage (Tokyo to Anchorage) by Broye (sic) Lafayette De Mente (b. Mo., 1928)."

But what happened to Elinore? And who, in heaven's name, is Broye Lafayette De Mente (b. Mo, 1928)?

###

Author's Note

Here is part of my response to Hilton's *CAR and DRIVER* article:

February 1986
Don Sherman,
Editor CAR and DRIVER
3460 Wilshire Blvd Los Angeles, Ca 90010

Dear Don:
I was delighted to see that Half-Safe, the globe-girdling amphibious jeep, made your AMAZING STORIES (Jan. 1986).

I was disappointed, however, that the story ended on a note of mystery—and that I was part of that mystery.

Years ago I provided the *Guinness Book of World Records* with an account of the Pacific crossing, but for some reason they have not seen fit to update the material.

To clear up some of your questions, Elinore, Ben Carlin's American wife, jumped jeep in India—no longer able to put up with either the Half-Safe or Carlin—and eventually got a divorce.

Since it was essential that he have a mate (the nautical kind), Carlin flew to Perth, Australia (his hometown) and recruited a young yachtsman to join the adventure. This young man lasted until the Half-Safe reached Kagoshima on the southern tip of Kyushu, Japan, in late 1956.

At that time, I was a resident of Japan, working as the editor of *Today's Japan* magazine and concurrently serving on the staff of *The Japan Times*.

Carlin drove the jeep up the Japanese island chain, arriving in Tokyo in November. There, he rented a room and settled in to wait for the following spring before attempting to cross the stormy North Pacific—and to find a new partner.

I interviewed Carlin, and found him to be an Australian redneck who was further handicapped by having spent several years in China and India, prior to and during World War II. He was, however, a master mechanic and navigator.

Carlin began advertising for a mate. There were no takers. In February 1957 he called me and asked me if I would like to take an ocean voyage (I had told him about having been in the Navy, and liking the sea). His only condition was that I learn how to operate one of his cameras, and that I not write about the voyage for five years after it was completed.

In the meantime, Carlin spent several weeks at the Shell Oil Company plant between Tokyo and Yokohama, working on a hugh torpedo-shaped tank that was to serve as a floating gasoline supply and be pulled behind Half-Safe on a long tow-line.

Despite holding down two full-time jobs in Tokyo at the time, I was not making very good money [and had some personal ties I wanted to break!]. Half-Safe provided not only the way, but offered an opportunity to participate in a genuine world-class adventure. I said yes.

We left Tokyo on May 3rd, 1957, heading north toward Hokkaido . . . . .

###

Letter from a CAR & DRIVER Reader

8 April 1986
Boye Lafayette De Mente,
Paradise Valley, Az 85253

Dear Mr. De Mente:

Reading your CAR and DRIVER (April 1986) article about the Half-Safe adventure was a pleasure, indeed. It brought back memories of events I had not thought of in years. United Seamen's Service, Inc., in New York employed me as a Field Representative (read seamen's club assistant manager) in various parts.

Between 1 May 1956 and 31 January 1957, I was at the USS Center in Naha, Okinawa. It was there that Ben Carlin and the young Australian, whose name I do not remember, came ashore practically in our front yard, arousing great curiosity.

They put the amphibian in our parking lot, where it remained for about two weeks, as I recall. They made the seamen's club their headquarters while there and got to know our staff, customers, and a crowd of press types, civilian and military functionaries, and other locals.

The Half-Safe and its crew attracted no end of attention. Carlin was the one who did most of the talking. The younger man did say he had enjoyed his journey and planned to continue, but it was possible to detect a certain lack of enthusiasm in his demeanor. Later we heard that he had bailed out when the couple got to Japan. I did not learn the end of the story until seeing your account of it.

Carlin had a supply of his books about the first part of the adventure, when his wife was with him. He left them to be sold at the seamen's club, but the price was so high that no one bought any. I regret that I did not keep even one. When I was transferred to Guam in February 1957 the books were still on hand and I never heard any more about them. They may be there yet.

If you publish more about this I would like to hear about it. Reading your account in C&D was a treat.

Cordially, Van A. Stilley, Attorney At Law

###

On June 2, 1986, Perth's *Daily News* ran an update on the Half-Safe, written by Allan Hale, with a photograph of the jeep showing it on display at the Guildford Grammar School. The story was headlined:

ATLANTIC CROSSING OF FAMOUS OLD JEEP

A stubby vehicle, painted in yellow and red, is parked under glass in a new handicraft complex opened today at Guildford Grammar School.

"I wouldn't drive it across the Swan River," said the builder of the craft centre and the glass case, Mr. Gerry Tangey (33). He would have been in diapers when somebody drove it across the Atlantic.

Six metres long, man-high, standing on four wheels and with a single small propeller aft, it is a relic of one of the most foolhardy enterprises the world has ever seen and which today is in danger of being entirely forgotten.

The war-surplus 1942 modified amphibious Ford Jeep is a monument to do-it-yourself. In 1956 a Guildford old boy once drove the toy-like thing across the Atlantic from Nova Scotia to Africa.

His name was Ben Carlin, and he sounds quite a man. When he died, in 1981, he left the school shares worth $ 100,000 to encourage Latin and "cliche-free English." The shares subsequently sky-rocketed and the school remembers him fondly.

"When he made the trip in 1956, it was headline news round the world," says school development officer Mr. Mike Ferrier." Somebody the other day had never heard of him."

Carlin wrote a book, *Half-Safe*, about the enterprise which is listed in the *Guinness Book of Records*. The vehicle was recovered from America in 1984.

###

27 July 1986
Dear Mr. De Mente
"ONCE A FOOL"

As mentioned by telephone to your office, I wonder if you are willing to sell me two of the remaining copies of "Once a Fool?"

I would also welcome any news of a reprint or new edition of this title. As a publisher, I wonder if you would have any interest in Carlin's manuscript (never published) of the Pacific section of his circumnavigation. I think it would be accessible to me, though I have never seen it, and only assume it covers the continuation of "Half-Safe".

An International Reply Coupon is enclosed. Yours sincerely, D J Shephard, Devon, England.

#

On June 27, 1987 *The West Australian* carried a story about Ben Carlin's daughter, Deirdre, showing up in Perth on a "sentimental journey." The piece, written by Hugh Schmitt, added another dimension to the saga of the Half-Safe:

Daughter's Sentimental Journey

The memory of a famous father who made an incredible journey 30 years ago has brought Deirdre Carlin to Perth on a sentimental journey.

Her father, Major Ben Carlin, who died at Cottesloe in March, 1981, was the only man to have circumnavigated the world in an amphibious jeep—called Half-Safe. The Northam-born adventurer braved storms, currents, tides, mountains, deserts and jungles to sail 9600 nautical miles and motor 62,5000 kilometres between 1951 and 1958.

Deirdre Carlin, who saw the father she craved to get to know only once—when she was three—found it an emotional experience to hear her father's voice on the soundtrack of a film she has discovered and to sit in the restored vehicle.

The jeep, painted a vivid yellow with red trim, now sits in a glass display house at Guildford Grammar School where Ben Carlin was educated.

"I was only a few months old when my mother, who was only 21, left my father, then 52, taking me with her," recalls the Arlington, Virginia-born daughter in a cultured English accent— she was educated at a boarding school in Madeira.

"I was virtually kidnapped. I tried several times to correspond with my father and he tried often to get letters to me, but my mother blocked our efforts to get in touch.

"I did get a letter from him from Cottesloe when I was 14, but my mother urged me not to respond to it. She was always poisoning me against him."

At 17, she again wrote to her father but she received a reply from a neighbor saying that Ben Carlin had died two months earlier.

The square-jawed adventurer, a mining engineer by profession, left most of his sizeable estate to his alma mater to endow a scholarship.

While living on Cottesloe, Major Carlin offered Half-Safe— he was then co-owner with an American friend—to the Fremantle Maritime museum, but the museum rejected the historic vehicle saying it had nowhere to display it.

Major Carlin then bequeathed his share of Half-Safe to Guildford Grammar, whose school foundation bought out the American partner and brought the jeep to Perth.

The school also has other Carlin memorabilia—logbooks, sextant, pictures—in its archives. Says Guildford Grarnmar headmaster, Mr. J . M. Moody, (father of the State cricketer):

"The Half-Safe display is a nonverbal testimony to a man's dedication and sense of adventure and is an example for present-day students to follow."

Major Carlin told the late *Daily News* columnist Kirwan Ward in 1974: "I could drive Half-Safe now from Perth to Sydney without any trouble at all."

Deirdre Carlin, who has hundreds of yellowing press clippings about her famous father, was persuaded by his neighbors and friends to make the trip to Perth.

"I intended to come last year, but my mother died in August, so I put the trip off," she says.

"I felt quite daunted when I arrived, but my father' s friends have made me feel really at home. It's amazing the number of people I've met who knew him.

"When I saw the film my father made of his voyage and heard his voice it was an incredibly emotional experience."

Miss Carlin also has a manuscript for a second book her father wrote on his amazing journey. The first book, *Half-Safe*, made the best-seller lists round the world.

"The second book is quite thick, but it summarizes the first book, which told only of Half-Safe's voyage across the Atlantic, which he shared with his first wife Elinore," she explains.

Deirdre Carlin has "met" her late father's cat, Puddy Cat, who since his death has lived with a family friend, Mrs. Beatrice Bonnerup, of Mundaring.

Author's Note

My old friend, John Rohrbough whom I met on Shemya Island, still in Perth, saw the above story, contacted Deirdre Carlin, and gave her my address in Tokyo. She wrote me the following:

29 June 1987
Mr. Boyé De Mente c/o Japan Journal, Tokyo 160, Japan

Dear Mr. De Mente:
I have just spoken to John Rohrbough who gave me your address, etc. I was very pleased to hear from him, as I am hoping to get the second manuscript published. The second

book incorporates the departure from England, through Europe and Asia, to India, Japan, the Pacific, Alaska back to Montreal, as you probably know.

Barry Hanley (who accompanied my Father from India to Japan) is currently in Perth. I have a couple of copies of the manuscript but we (myself and Guildford Grammar School, the sole beneficiary of my Father's estate) assume that a certain doctor in the USA considers that he has rights to the copyright of the second book.

My friend and representative from Guildford, Mr. David Malcolm QC will be visiting the USA within the next couple of weeks, so I hope that he will be able to resolve the matter then.

I have been in Perth for 4 months now. Things have been very slow indeed with regard to sorting this all out (hindered mainly by the doctors non-reply to all of David's letters since 1983!). The enclosed article has already been of use (ie attracting John Rohrbough to call), so it is great. A couple of points are slightly "spiced up"-poetic license, I suppose. I look forward to hearing from you, as and when.

Yours Sincerely, Deirdre (Carlin)

Author's Note

My response to Deirdre Carlin was as diplomatic as possible under the circumstances, but I had no qualms about letting her know that my view of her "famous" father was quite different from the news reports and from the comments of friends who had never spent months with him cooped up in a tiny ocean-going jeep.

During this same flurry of interest caused by the *Car and Driver* article, I also heard from Elinore Carlin, Ben's first wife who made the Atlantic crossing with him and hung on until India (several years later). Now a business woman, she came through to me as a warm and talented lady with a great sense of humor.

————————————————

CONTENTS

The Meeting
Leaving Tokyo
On the Road
The First Water
Wakkanai: Jumping Off Point
Underway the First Time
Underway the Second Time
Underway and Out of Contact
Living in a Coma
The Yellow Monster
The Kurile Islands
Trapped in a Kelp Field
Into the North Pacific
Visitors from Russia
Gassing Up in Rough Water
The First Collision
The Second Collision
Taking Preventive Action
Asleep at the Wheel
The Creeping Wall
The Happiest Day
A New Crisis
The Playful Walruses
Over the Side
First Land
A Nine-Day Break
To Sea Again
The Art of Navigation
Commotion on Adak Island

Through the Boiling Sea
Adventures on Umnak
Smooth Sailing and Whales
Stop-Over at Unalaska
More Smooth Sailing
At Cold Cold Bay
Shooting Shellikof Straits
Kodiak and the Deserted Cove
Dolphins in the Night
I Avoid a Collision
The Sunning Seals
Surprise on Homer's Spit
Breaching Cook Inlet
The Last of the Sea
Anchorage and the End

(1)
The Meeting

For me the story of Half-Safe began with a news story that appeared in *The Japan Times* in Tokyo in the fall of 1956. Ben Carlin, Australian skipper of the amphibious jeep—in which he was circling the globe—had lost his latest partner and was in need of a new one.

For those who may not have heard of the Half-Safe and its captain, a little background will clear up the mystery.

While still in the Royal Indian Engineers in India in 1946, Carlin happened to run across a number of amphibious jeeps—some of the thousands of American service vehicles then in the process of being turned over to the Indian Government.

Being of a sporting nature and having a wry sense of humor, Carlin suggested that with a bit of doing, one could go around the world in such a vehicle.

His companion at the time—whom Carlin admits was both intelligent and practical—questioned the feasibility of the idea. This was enough to convince Carlin that not only could it be done but that he was the man to do it. He estimated that the whole trip would take around twelve months.

Upon his discharge from the military in August 1946, Carlin departed for the United States in search of a surplus jeep. He found one, finally got ownership of it, renovated and outfitted it for an extended sea voyage, nearly killed himself testing it, married an American girl and finally debarked from New York—with his new American wife as second in command—in June 1948. Their goal: the west coast of Africa by way of the Azores.

Four days later they limped back into the mouth of New Jersey's Shark River, having been beset by a raft of problems that made continuing unthinkable. In mid-July they made two more starts that ended in quick failure. On the 7th of August they were off again. On the 8th day out, the propeller shaft thrust bearing went bad. On the 18th day—after 10 days of drifting helplessly—they and the jeep were picked up by a freighter and taken to Montreal, Canada. After cleaning the jeep, they drove the 900 miles to Halifax, Nova Scotia.

Nearly two years later, on the 19th of July 1950, the repaired Half-Safe once again put to sea; this time successfully.

On the 19th of August, the 32nd day, after enough problems and mishaps to last several men a life-time, the Carlin's arrived in Flores, the Azores. Then followed a series of island hops which were marked by several near fatal events and long layovers for repairs and recuperation.

Finally on the 23rd of February 1951, the Half-Safe trundled ashore at Cap Juby, Africa. It had taken the Carlin' s six months, but they had crossed the Atlantic Ocean in a vehicle about the size of a compact car and half the size of the smallest powered vessel ever to have made the crossing before.

From Cap Juby, the Carlin's drove overland on a circular route across a portion of the Spanish Sahara, then up the African Coastline through French Morocco by way of Casablanca, Tangier and Gibraltar. At Gibraltar they crossed the straits to Portugal, and then on land again went on through Spain to France.

From Paris, the Carlin's took the Half-Safe sightseeing to Brussels, Hamburg and on to Malmo in distant Sweden. They then doubled back and at Brussels crossed the English Channel. The Half-Safe arrived in the center of London on Sunday the 26th of August 1951, almost exactly one year from the date of its departure from Halifax.

It took Carlin two and a half years to get Half-Safe back in shape for the second lap of its amazing journey. Except for the engine, he completely rebuilt the jeep. But one delay after the other kept the Carlin's bogged down in London until 1956.

When they did get underway they made relatively good time overland to Istanbul, Damascus, Bagdad, Teheran, Kabul and Calcutta.

In India there was a mutiny. Carlin's second in command, his wife, gave up the ship. She was replaced by a young Australian who managed to endure as far as Japan, where he also decamped.

I had never considered myself particularly brave. In fact, I used to wonder if my courage would measure up that of the ordinary man. But in this case there was a woman I could compare myself to: Carlin's wife.

If she could do it, I told myself, so could I. It is my judgment now that Mrs. Carlin must have been a very extraordinary woman. I was to learn through experience, both bitter and sweet, that Carlin was an extraordinary man.

Carlin had rented rooms in a Japanese home in the Takanawa section of Tokyo to wait until spring, since crossing the North Pacific in an amphibious jeep during winter was inconceivable.

I telephoned him and he suggested I come to see him at his apartment. Because it was impossible to pinpoint the location of the house he was staying in, he agreed to meet me at an easy-to-find intersection in the vicinity. A Japanese friend who had recently acquired a used Renault drove me to the meeting.

It was a cold, windy day. Not many people were on the street when we arrived at the appointed place, but it took us some time to spot Carlin. Finally we saw him standing up close to a corner building to get out of the wind.

We left the car and walked toward him. He did not present a very striking figure. He was dressed in faded corduroy trousers and a nondescript coat, had sandy brown hair and a short stubble of red beard. He looked like a seaman off of some tramp ship.

At his apartment Carlin showed my friend and I some of his pictures and some magazines that had carried stories of the

Atlantic crossing. He asked me a few questions about myself, and displayed particular interest in whether or not I knew how to use cameras. I told him I had had the usual amateur experiences. When my friend and I took our leave after a short while, Carlin asked that I call him a few weeks later for his answer on whether or not he wanted me to join him on the trip.

I called at the arranged time and was told that I had been selected. I do not think I had very much competition. At our next meeting, Carlin gave me some instructions on how to use his cameras, and I practiced dry runs on them for about half an hour. When I left his apartment this time he loaned me a copy of his book telling about the conception of the idea, the preparation and the crossing of the Atlantic.

During the following winter months we met some four or five times; once again at his apartment, once at mine, once to see the jeep when he took it out of the basement garage of a member of the Australian Embassy in Japan, and then once when he went to the Kawasaki depot of Standard Vacuum Oil Company to drive the Half-Safe back to Tokyo.

Carlin had taken the jeep to the depot earlier to tune it up for the overland trip to Hokkaido. At the depot he had also constructed a long, cigar-shaped gas tank which we were to pull behind us at the end of a rope when we finally put to sea.

When Carlin invited me to go with him to pick up the jeep, I asked if it would be all right to take a girl friend along. He agreed readily. It was a Sunday, and when we arrived at the depot there was no one around. Carlin went directly to where he had parked the jeep—out in the open. It wasn't there. At just this moment, one of the Japanese executives of the oil company, who was out driving with his family, pulled up and began explaining to Carlin that he was the one who had moved Half-Safe—to get it out of the rain.

Carlin's face turned red and he began to tremble with fury. "You brainless ass! You bloody bastard!" he railed wildly. "Who told you you could touch that jeep?"

The Japanese man was shocked, embarrassed and confused. He looked from his family to my girl friend, to me and back to Carlin.

"No one told me to move the jeep, but it started to rain..." he managed to get out before Carlin cut him off again.

For what seemed like a short eternity Carlin continued to abuse the man, finally ending up by telling him several times that he (Carlin) was going to lodge an official complaint with the man's foreign superior. The outburst was as much of a surprise and shock to me as it was to the unfortunate Japanese.

But it shouldn't have been. I had read Carlin's book and should have been better prepared for this type of reaction from him. I at least had the sense to recognize the incident as a portent of what I was letting myself in for. But, like Caesar, my die was cast.

Half-Safe's engine kicked over and commenced with a powerful roar at the first touch of the starter button. Then with Carlin at the wheel we began threading our way carefully into Tokyo.

But we were not quite careful enough. We had not been on the main highway very long when we were side-swiped by a bus—fortunately only lightly. It was still cold—it had snowed earlier that morning—and we rode inside the jeep with the hatch cover down. The steady roar of the engine in the enclosed cabin made conversation a severe strain, and we were mostly silent all the way back to Tokyo.

As I was to later learn only too well, the constant throbbing din of the engine was a blessing in disguise. My friend and I left Carlin and the jeep as soon as he arrived at his destination.

After we had parted from Carlin, my girl-friend turned to me and said: "You're not as smart as I thought you were!"

The Departure from Tokyo

Spring was late in coming to Tokyo in 1957 and it was the 3rd of May before we got underway. Earlier Carlin had applied to the Russian Embassy in Tokyo for permission to stop over at a Soviet port on the Siberian peninsula of Kamchatka.

Despite a number of follow-up letters after he submitted the request, there was nothing from the Russians but ominous silence. When I left my apartment that morning, I cannot say I was disappointed that the application had been ignored.

I had very few preparations to make, and outwardly there was no indication I was about to embark on a remarkable adventure. My friends had tired of telling me I was crazy. In late March I had come down with pneumonia and was still some 14 pounds underweight.

On the morning set for our departure, I met Carlin at the home of some of his Australian friends where he had spent the last few days. The jeep was there, and it took only a few minutes to store my small plastic suitcase, half-filled sea-bag and portable typewriter (which I was to sell while en route to Hokkaido) in the bit of space remaining behind the area that served as sleeping quarters.

I had arranged, with Carlin's approval, that we would officially leave from the front of the *Mainichi* Newspaper Building in downtown Tokyo at 10 o'clock that morning. It was 9 o'clock before we left the home of Carlin's friends.

A stop at a nearby post office took up another twenty minutes. Then we drove to the American Embassy apartments where Carlin had arranged to buy some things such as kleenex from the small PX shop maintained there for diplomatic personnel. It was after 10 before we got away from the apartments.

A combination of what surely must be the world's most labyrinthian streets, congested traffic and poor visibility from the driver's seat of the jeep added up to nearly an hour for the short run from the embassy store to the Mainichi Building. It was 11 o'clock when we arrived there to find a large crowd waiting.

I learned later that as the result of an announcement of the jeep's departure in the previous day's newspaper, the crowd had begun gathering in front of the building at 7 o'clock that morning.

The *Mainichi* had photographers posted on ladders near where the jeep was supposed to stop, and there were also several hanging out of second and third story windows. Most of the crowd also had cameras. As soon as we pulled in, shutters began to click by the hundreds.

When the jeep stopped, I climbed out of the tank-like cabin and sat with my legs dangling through the open hatchway. I expected Carlin to join me immediately so everyone could take pictures of us. But he didn't. He remained in the jeep, hidden from all except those who could get close enough to peer through the small windows.

"Aren't you coming out?" I called to him.

"When I get ready," he replied laconically.

I looked in to see what he was doing. He was loading film into one of his several cameras, and had several more to go. He passed his Leica 35mm up to me and told me to load it. I opened the camera and began fumbling with the film. In the excitement it was two or three minutes before I realized there was no empty spool in the camera.

I asked Carlin to pass one up to me. He couldn't find one and suggested I borrow one from a Mainichi photographer. A cameraman tossed one down to me from a second floor window.

All during this time, dozens of people were yelling for both of us to come out of the jeep. Others were indiscriminately calling out questions which I relayed to Carlin and then translated his answers into Japanese. I was all thumbs and couldn't get the Leica loaded. I finally gave up and passed it down to Carlin.

"I'm sorry. I can't do it with this crowd bothering me," I said.

If there had been the slightest possibility of him finding a replacement for me at that late date, I'm sure Carlin would have told me to get my "bloody ass" out of his sight. He was proudest of his ability with his hands, and had the vilest contempt for anyone who was less skilled than he.

By this time we had been parked in front of the Mainichi for about fifteen minutes, but it seemed like hours to me. Carlin was still loading cameras and puttering around inside the Jeep—deliberately, I thought, delaying his emergence just to demonstrate his independence to the shouting crowd.

The *Mainichi* executives with whom I had arranged the press coverage were beginning to chaff. One of them kept yelling down to me, "What's wrong? What's wrong?" About the fifth time I replied that Carlin was still putting film into his cameras, the answer began to sound silly.

Finally, Carlin came out, favored me with a dour look and proceeded to take his own pictures from our vantage point high on the jeep. Then he posed for a few minutes, waving his hand in the air as if saying farewell and smiling a cold smile.

Carlin (standing) and De Mente on Half-Safe in front of the Mainichi Newspaper Building in downtown Tokyo, May 3, 1957.

I didn't blame him by this time. I was tired of the crowd too, and I'd been exposed to it for less than half an hour. He had been putting up with the same thing on and off for nine years.

When Carlin decided enough pictures had been taken, he slid into the hatchway, started up the engine and drove slowly through the crowd massed in the street. I thought we were on our way, but I finally realized we were following a small car on some sort of pre-arranged route around the grounds in front of the Imperial Palace.

Then instead of heading out of the city, the little car led us back through Yurakucho to the Ginza and up to the Yomiuri Newspaper Building. To my surprise, there was another recaption committee waiting for us, including a number of foreign correspondents.

We went through the picture-taking routine again, and were more or less interviewed by some of the correspondents. My lady friend, who had gone to Kawasaki with Carlin and me, was present and because she was obviously a close friend soon got involved in the affair.

A woman reporter, spying what she though was a new angle, asked the girl if she was Mrs. De Mente. The excited girl said "yes."

To avoid later complications, I suggested to both the young lady and the reporter that okusan (wife) be amended to "fiancé."

Carlin appeared to enjoy the little byplay. The stop at the Yomiuri was a short one and within minutes we were actually on the road—still following the small car which had pick us up after we left the Mainichi. Strung out behind the jeep were several other cars filled with friends, news photographers and people attracted by the odd sight we made.

With Carlin driving—as it turned out he always did while we were on land—we made it to what might be called the outskirts of Tokyo in about an hour. There we stopped, took leave of most of the people who had followed us, then went into a small noodle shop with the few close friends who remained, and ate our first meal on the road.

Eating noodles on the outskirts of Tokyo, our first stop on the road.

It was at this point I discovered the small car leading us belonged to a Japanese staff member of Stanvac Oil Company. In return for a small amount of assistance from the oil firm, Carlin had agreed to stop briefly at the company's various gasoline stations along our route to Hokkaido as a publicity gimmick.

The man in the little car was to be our front man until we reached a certain station, then he would be replaced by someone else. In all, we were to have company as far as Aomori, our jumping off point for Hokkaido.

On The Road

The next few days were fairly routine. Once or twice a day we would arrive in a town where there was a Stanvac station. If it was early in the day we would stop there for a few hours and then drive on to the next town. Our schedule had been arranged so we would arrive in a town with a station late in the afternoon, and there we would stay the night—usually as guests of the station operator.

Local newspapers and radio stations had been notified of our schedule, and carried a running account of our progress. As a result there was a crowd waiting for us at each station. The crowd took pictures of us and the jeep, and Carlin took pictures of the crowd. Then there would be a question and answer period.

The questions were always the same: what did we eat; where did we sleep; how fast would the jeep go; what did we do to pass the time at sea?

At first I translated all the questions into English for Carlin's benefit, and gave only answers that he supplied. This soon became boring for both of us—quite often he wouldn't say anything appropriate anyway—and I finally stopped referring the questions to Carlin unless they pertained only to him.

Somewhere along the line it was suggested we drive the jeep to the local school grounds after we had made our usual stop at a station. For sometime afterward, this was standard procedure if our departure from a station was during school hours. But the practice was stopped following an incident which surely surprised, and probably mystified as well, a large number of people.

After leaving a station in a certain city and driving to one school ground, Carlin was prevailed upon by the oil company representative with us and various school officials to visit a second school before leaving the city. We were to follow behind the car of some of the people involved. But instead of guiding us directly to the school, the driver began leading us on a tour through a part of the city that was hilly and had narrow, twisting streets heavily congested with traffic.

After about half an hour of this (by which time our numbers had grown to caravan size) and a number of near accidents with the jeep, Carlin got fed up. By coincidence, the caravan leaders began taking us across a main thoroughfare which Carlin recognized as the highway out of the city. Without warning, he broke out of the line of vehicles and cut out down the highway.

We were on the outskirts of the city several miles away when our oil company man caught up with us, pulled out in front of Half-Safe and tried to flag us down. Carlin sped on past him without a sign. At our next stop, the man apologized for allowing the school visit to degenerate into a circus.

A day or so after this we had no scheduled stop in the evening, and it was decided to put up a well-known spa a few miles off our course. By this time we had picked up a new oil company representative; a young man who took his responsibilities to us seriously.

It was already late in the evening by the time we arrived at the spa. We went directly to one of the leading inns, which was built on the side of a gorge so most of the floors were down instead of up. Carlin and I were put into a typical Japanese suite on the first floor below the lobby. Our road companion was lodged next door to us.

Bath time was announced immediately. Carlin and I traded our dust-impregnated clothes for crisply starched yukata (robes) and headed for the hot water-taking along a bottle of gin to keep us company. The combination of hot water and gin lifted our spirits and restored a degree of comradeship which had been conspicuously missing since our departure from Tokyo.

Shortly after we returned to our suite, a Japanese meal accompanied by numerous bottles of beer was served by several giggling maids. We made a regular party of it for the next hour. Afterward, I elected to go to bed. Carlin decided to go out on the town with our young Japanese man. They left and I crawled into my sleeping mats.

The next thing I recall is being abruptly awakened by someone falling over me. The lights in the room were suddenly turned on. Standing in the middle of the floor was Carlin, still in his yukata and with all his sheets to the wind, so to speak.

The body that had fallen over me was a girl in her late teens or early twenties, also dress in a yukata. Carlin had apparently shoved her down on me and was all set to do it again if need be.

"It's your turn now, mate ! " he announced, pushing the half-risen girl back across my legs with his foot.

The girl began shouting invective at Carlin. He kept yelling at me to grab her. I told him I didn't think she was in the mood. He insisted that didn't make any difference, and pulled his yukata aside to show me his red, bruised knees.

"You don't think I got these shooting craps, do you?" he yelled.

About this time our oil man dashed into the room and began trying to drag Carlin away from the girl. Up to this time, Carlin had been shoving her back down with his foot every time she attempted to get up. The oil man was joined by several maids who began trying to pacify the screaming girl.

Finally I leaned back on one elbow and began watching the scene as if I had nothing to do with it whatsoever.

After a short struggle, Carlin saw it was useless and gave up with such grace I was amazed. He looked at me, winked, and said "It's your loss, mate." Then he disappeared into the hallway.

There followed several minutes of apologizing by the maids and the oil man to the girl in the yukata. She told them to go to hell, got up and stalked out. Then they turned and began apologizing to me. I apologized to them. It was half an hour before I got back to sleep.

The next morning Carlin was in his sleeping mats in the room connected with mine. He was a few minutes longer than usual in getting out of bed, but the fact that he was able to get out at all was astounding. We ate a late breakfast, and got underway a little after 10 o'clock.

Our oil man was gone and we were to see no more of him. Carlin suffered his hangover in silence for several hours. I rode on top of the jeep until the wind turned cold. Then I went below and encouraged him to talk about Australia—a safe enough topic since I could just sit back and listen. Carlin loved to lecture.

A few hours before we arrived in Morioka, the capital of Iwate Prefecture, we passed through a number of small towns and villages in which racial mixtures between the Japanese and Ainu (the aboriginal inhabitants of the Japanese islands) became evident in a particularly shocking way.

Each place we stopped, Half-Safe acted like a magnet on young children, drawing them as lights do moths. Within minutes of our arrival we could count on a crowd of at least twenty-five kids ranging in age from one to seven or eight. Most of them would stand back several feet from the jeep and stare at us solemnly. If we were still inside the jeep, a few were always brave enough to come closer and peer at us through the windows.

The first evidence I saw of Ainu blood was in a girl about seven years old. I was immediately attracted to her extraordinary large, light brown eyes and fair complexion. When I was able to get a closer look at her, I noticed one of her eyes was slightly crossed. As soon as she became conscious of my stare she turned and ran away.

At our next stop that same morning, there were at least three kids in the crowd that gathered around us who were mixed-bloods. All had wonderfully fair skin, light brown eyes and brownish hair. One was a boy about three, and the other two were girls. Both of the little boy's eyes were badly crossed. One of the girls had a crossed eye, and one of the eyes of the last girl had begun to wither away.

The further we got into Iwate, the more mixed children we saw, and the higher rose the percentage of those who had at least one crossed or malformed eye. Since we were passing through the towns during working hours, not many adults were attracted to the jeep.

I began to observe more closely the few who did show up. In each crowd there was at least one Japanese-Ainu with the same or similar eye defect I had seen in the children—only in the adults it was worse. Instead of an eye just being crossed, it seemed that as the people grew older their one bad eye gradually withered away until there was nothing left but a tiny slit in a shallow depression.

The eyes of all the Japanese-Ainu I saw whether they were bad or not, were considerably farther apart than any I had ever seen before. Some were so far apart it made the people appear grotesque, and I noticed the farther apart the eyes were the more likely it was for one of them to be deformed.

In Sendai we were treated to a party in an entertainment district and there were all kinds of hints we were going to be fixed up with "instant wives" but nothing came of it. The rest of the trip to Aomori, where I was to get my first taste of the jeep at sea, was uneventful.

In Aomori, things were to liven up a bit. Being a large and important city, our oil company contact in Aomori was a more substantial businessman than most of those we had so far met.

As a result we were soon comfortably accommodated in a first class inn and found ourselves with several invitations to go out on the town that night. We were to get the jeep ready to go into the water the following day and embark when the weather and tide were favorable.

Since turning Half-Safe from a land vehicle to a sea-craft consisted of attaching the propeller and rudder—a job requiring less than an hour—we had very little to do, and accepted one of the invitations.

That night found us in a popular cabaret. When closing time came the party split up. Carlin asked to be dropped off at our inn, while I joined two of our hosts and several of the cabaret girls at an all-night bar in another part of the city. About 2 a.m. this party started breaking up, and shortly afterward I was back at our lodgings with one of our original hosts and two cabaret girls in tow.

Everyone at the inn was asleep and we had to make a lot of noise before a maid finally got up and unlocked the front door. She had given me up and no longer expected me to come back, much less have three people with me. She didn't know what to do. Eventually a second maid got up and fortunately happened to know the man who was with me. She led him and one of the girls away, and I never saw them again.

Finally I asked the first maid to lead me and the remaining girl to Carlin's room. I didn't intend to offer him the same opportunity he had presented to me a few days previously, but there didn't appear to be any other choice, and I didn't want to spend the remaining few hours of the night sitting in a cold, dark lobby.

Very reluctantly, it seemed, the maid led us to Carlin's room. He was asleep. Along side of his bedding was a second mat that had been laid out for me. Both myself and the girl had been drinking beer for several hours and should have been sleepy. But we had apparently got our second wind and were in the mood to start another party.

Our talking woke Carlin up. He snarled at us, rolled over and covered up his head. We were saved from further imposing on his hospitality by the reappearance of the maid with the news she had found a vacant room and would serve us there.

It was 5 o'clock when I dozed off. Much to my relief, the day broke windy and cold, and Carlin decided to wait for better weather before attempting to cross the Tsugaru Strait separating the main island of Honshu from Hokkaido.

But the following morning brought more of the same weather, and once again our departure was postponed. On the fourth morning it was more promising. By shortly before noon, the wind had almost completely died.

Carlin passed the word we were leaving. We returned to the inn from the gasoline station to pick up the few belongings we had left there. While we were gathering up our things, the maids brought us separate bills.

"Isn't Mr So & So going to take care of this?" we asked in surprise.

Up to that time we had assumed we were guests of the local oil company representative, since he had made all arrangements for us without our knowledge or approval, and there had been other incidents to indicate such was the case.

The maids acted even more surprised than we did. They disappeared, taking the bills with them. I knew they had gone to call our supposed benefactor. A few minutes later they returned, this time very much embarrassed, and said that since we were really not the guests of Mr. So & So, we would have to pay our own bills.

We promptly paid, much to the relief of the maids, but were not too happy with our host of the last few days, because we would not have put up in such expensive lodgings on our own accord.

The First Water

It was only a few minutes drive from the gas station where Half-Safe was parked to the beach area where we intended to go into the water. Several carloads of people left the station with us. By the time we got near the beach we had picked up another dozen cars. Our place of departure had been announced on radio and TV, and there was also a crowd waiting for us at the beach.

Many of the people who had come to see us off had left their cars blocking the final approach to the beach, and it took nearly half an hour to clear a way for us. Once we gained the beach we began preparations for attaching the propeller and rudder. This was delayed several times by the crowd, especially the children, pushing in so close our movements were hampered.

Attaching the rudder to Half-Safe's rear end.

Finally a group of young men affiliated with the gas station saved the day by shoving the crowd back, locking their arms and holding it off.

It was around 4 o'clock when we finally crawled in Half-Safe, drove slowly across the sand—so as not to run anyone down—and eased out into the water. By this time the sea appeared to us like a haven. Carlin turned to me and said "No matter how rough it may get at sea, at least you don' t have to put up with crowds!"

We entered the water at the head of Aomori Bay, and spent the next few hours with Tsugaru Peninsula about a mile to our left, and the yawning mouth of Mutsu Bay to our right.

Some time before darkness fell, it became obvious that we had sprung a leak somewhere in the bottom of the jeep. It became necessary to use the bilge pump every thirty minutes to keep Half-Safe from filling with water and sinking.

When we entered the open sea from Aomori Bay, the jeep began to buck and see-saw a little, but the movement wasn't unpleasant. A little further on, the see-saw motion changed to a sliding motion, as we began to go up and down larger waves. I had experienced a lot rougher rides in the streets of Tokyo, and it didn't bother me.

Steering the jeep, however, was another matter. Because of the short, squat body and small rudder, it was impossible to keep the jeep anywhere near on course without constantly adjusting the tiller right and left and back again. Even then, we did not move through the water in a straight line. We zig-zagged, veering from right to left and left to right. The degree of the deviation depended on the roughness of the water, the wind, and how conscientiously we applied ourselves to the tiller.

The only way to determine whether or not we were on course was to keep our eyes glued to a small compass hanging down from the overhead about two feet from the driver's face. This meant that in order to stay close to the course we could not look away from the compass for more than a split second at a time. As a result, we were moving completely blind most of the time.

To keep this up—staring wide-eyed at the compass and perpetually adjusting the tiller—was comparable to something like trying to ride a unicycle over a rough road without getting off a white line no wider than the thickness of a post-card. To do it the best it could be done was exhausting, physically and mentally, and after a while became excruciating torture.

We arrived at a little-used harbor on the outskirts of Hakodate about mid-afternoon the next day. On the way into the harbor we got out of the deep-water channel and too close to shore. Before we could recover and back off, Half-Safe began scraping bottom and careening off submerged rocks.

No damage was done, however, and a short while later we approached a concrete slipway intending to drive the jeep up on the beach. On our first approach we began drifting sideways. To prevent the jeep from bashing itself into the sharp side of the slipway, I jumped overboard into waist-deep water and pushed it away. The slipway itself was fairly steep.

After reconsidering for a few minutes, Carlin decided to try driving up on a sandy beach a few hundred yards south of the harbor. In order for us to approach this area of the beach from the sea it was necessary to go some distance around an oil-pipe platform that extended from the shore out to where the water was deep enough to take large tankers. The wind was blowing off-shore and there was a current running seaward.

With our top speed only about four miles an hour, we would have to get up considerable momentum to get through the surf and far enough in so the wheels could get a grip on the hard-packed sandy bottom.

With Carlin at the tiller, I stationed myself on the bow of the jeep and held the loose end of a tow line, ready to jump overboard in case we got into shallow water and the jeep started swinging sideways—in which position in might capsize.

Our arrival at the harbor had been expected, and by that time our reception committee was on the beach waiting for us to come in. A motor boat also appeared and got a little too close for Carlin's comfort. He popped his head out of the hatchway and shouted "Stand off you bloody asses ! Are you trying to ram us?"

I'm sure no one on the boat understood the meaning of Carlin's words but they got the idea, and the boat moved away a hundred yards or more. Carlin then revved up the engine and we headed for the beach. We were fairly flying (for an amphibious jeep) and everything went well until we were about fifty yards out.

Then Half-Safe began to bounce as if we were running wild down a boulder-strewn mountainside. The bottom that far out was rocky, and the front wheels of the jeep were slamming into the rocks. An especially vicious collision threw the jeep sideways so we were running parallel to the beach. The transmission was still in propeller drive.

Carlin gave the jeep full left rudder and we headed back out into deep water.

Once again we lined up with the shore and made a run for it. The same thing happened. We were circling for the third attempt when the engine began sputtering and finally coughed itself to death. We were out of gas. The jeep began drifting seaward.

Fortunately, the motor boat Carlin had ordered off was still close enough for us to hail it. At Carlin's request I told them we were out of gas and asked them to bring us a gallon or so in a can. They were gone about twenty minutes. By the time they got back we had drifted more than a mile out into the bay. While we were gassing up, one of the men on the motor boat suggested we approach the beach a little more to the right the next time where the bottom wasn't so rocky.

We took his advice, and the next attempt was successful. The change-over from propeller drive to wheel was accomplished with perfect coordination. We pulled up on the beach as easily as one drives into a parking lot. Carlin finally brought Half-Safe to a halt a few feet from hard-packed ground to avoid crashing into spectators blocking the way.

Leaving the jeep there on the beach with an old man watching over it, we accompanied more oil company representatives into Hakodate proper. Late that evening we went out to check on the jeep and gas up. The old man was gone and the incoming tide was lapping at the Half Safe' s wheels.

Carlin got in, started up and tried to pull further onto the beach, but the water had softened the sand, and at the first turn of the wheels they sank into it.

We began trying to dig the jeep out with our bare hands and a small shovel. No sooner would we scoop out a handful of sand than the rising waves would swirl in and fill it up again.

We kept this useless battle up for some twenty minutes. Finally I stopped in exasperation.

"We're not getting anywhere, Ben," I said.

Carlin bristled like a bayed wolf and snarled a line of curses at me. "If you would dig instead of talking, we might get somewhere, you god-damned stupid ass!" he shrieked.

Five minutes later he came to the same conclusion I had. Then someone in the crowd suggested we enlist the several dozen onlookers to pull the jeep out of its watery trap by rope. The same line I had made ready on our first landing attempt was strung out, willing hands grabbed it and began pulling energetically.

It took several attempts to get everyone to pull at the same time. As soon as this was accomplished, the jeep was quickly out on hard, dry land. By this time, however, it was completely dark. Rather than risk the rocks and other coastline dangers again, Carlin decided to layover the night in Hakodate. We stayed at the home of the local gas man.

It was close to noon when we got back to the jeep the next day. But getting into the water was always a lot easier than getting out, and we were soon heading eastward toward Shiokubi (Salt-Neck) Cape where we were to turn north and make for Muroran.

When we rounded the cape I was at the tiller and Carlin was asleep behind me. When I awoke him at the appointed time, the sea had turned choppy and Half-Safe was bucking like a mad bronco. Carlin stood up in the hatchway and surveyed the coastline for several minutes, now and then looking at his watch.

Then he ducked back into the cabin. "You stupid son-of-a-bitch! Where do you think you're going?" he screamed.

"To Muroran as far as I know," I answered. And then asked "Why?"

He had not given me a course-change before going to sleep, and from my low position in the cabin, I couldn't tell anything about our progress by looking out the window.

"Why? You bloody bastard! Why? Because you're off course, that's why!" His face was livid with rage.

"I'm on the course you gave me before you went to sleep. The same one you said to hold until I woke you!"

"I told you to change course after you'd been on that one for an hour! Now get on it!" he commanded, ending with a string of new invective.

I was just as disgusted with him as he was with me. "Look!" I said as calmly as possible. "If you had given me a change in course I'd know about it even if I wasn't on it. But you didn't. Now what course *am* I supposed to be on?"

Instead of answering me, Carlin leaned over, grasped the tiller over my hands and swung the jeep ninety degrees to the left. Within about half an hour we had left the choppy sea behind and were headed across the smooth mouth of Uchiura Bay toward Cape Etomo and Muroran.

It was mid-afternoon of the day after we left Hakodate when we began our approach to Muroran. Because of the position of the harbor behind Cape Etomo, ships have to make a sort of half circle around the cape and enter Muroran from the inward side of the bay.

With a draft of only a few feet, Carlin decided the Half-Safe could cut the circle short and save an hour or two. We cut it a little too short, however, and once again began colliding with submerged rocks.

Our slow speed saved us, but before we could find deeper water we hit so many boulders it seemed like we were determined to stove the jeep in. Working our way gingerly out of the shallow area, we finally got back into the regular ship channel and chugged on into Muroran.

There our re-conversion to an overland expedition was accomplished without incident. We drove up a nice, low-angled slipway that couldn't have been better if it had been built for us.

Removing the propeller and rudder and storing them back on top of the jeep required about thirty minutes. We then paid our respects to the local Stanvac agent, were treated to a bowl of noodles in a restaurant that had recently been converted from a whorehouse (we were just a few weeks late) and then turned Half-Safe northward toward Chitose.

There Carlin had a contact in one of the U.S. Forces installations, and had arranged to buy a supply of American-made color film. We arrived in the city late in the evening and put up at a small inn just a few hundred yards from the main entrance of the military camp. The next morning we called on Carlin's contact.

In addition to getting the film he wanted, we were interviewed by the Armed Forces Radio Service (AFRS) as well as a Chitose staff member of the Pacific Stars & Stripes.

An hour after leaving Chitose, we were in Sapporo, where a press luncheon had been arranged in our honor by the local agent of Stanvac. We were late and were rushed directly to the lunch meeting as soon as we arrived. The luncheon was very good and very impressive.

There were several dozen guests besides Carlin and myself, and about as many newsmen and photographers. During the interview that followed the meal, one of the reporters said he wanted to ask me an embarrassing question. I told him to go ahead.

"Is it really true" he asked, "That you and Carlin have been running out on your inn bills?"

I was stunned rather than embarrassed. "Certainly not!" I assured him. "Where in the hell did you hear that, anyway?" But I knew without asking.

Someone, maliciously or not, had given the press a garbled version of the mix-up in Aomori.

"It was reported from Aomori that you didn't pay your bills there," the newsman said.

"Well, we did!" I told him.

I could see my saying so hadn't convinced him or any of the other reporters listening in. Fortunately, I remembered Carlin stuffing the receipts for our bills into his wallet. I asked him for them and passed them around to all the reporters. This rather spoiled the rest of the luncheon and I wasn't sorry when it broke up.

By a few minutes to three we were on the road again with no planned stops until we reached Wakkanai on the northern tip of Hokkaido—from which Russian Saghalien could be seen on a clear day.

Wakkanai: Jumping Off Point

We made very good time for the next four hours, and decided to go on into Wakkanai that night. Just before dusk we had the first and only flat tire while I was aboard Half-Safe. This delayed us for around thirty minutes.

It was about 10 o'clock when, from a rise overlooking the crescent shaped Bay of Soya, we caught our first glimpse of Wakkanai. The city's lights, strung out along the inland coast of the bay, appeared like a string of stars that had somehow got snagged on the dark horizon.

With the instinct of a homing pigeon, Carlin drove directly to our gas station rendezvous. The lights were on in the station but it was closed, and it looked for a while like we were going to be on our own. But some banging on the door soon aroused an attendant. He called the oil company's Wakkanai depot and reported our arrival. A few minutes later a man drove down from the depot and guided us to it.

By now it was around midnight. A number of men lived in billets at the depot, and several of them got up to welcome us. Coffee was made, and we sat around a roaring coal fire and talked for more than an hour. There were several empty bunks in the billets, and the night manager of the depot invited Carlin and I to sleep there.

Although it was in the latter part of May by this time, the next morning dawned cold. The idea of setting our across the Sea of Okhotsk, the North Pacific and part of the Bering Sea was not a very pleasant prospect. But I need not have worried. We were not to get away that soon.

A methodical man, Carlin also had introductions to James Lowell, the Unit Commander of the U.S. military facility just north of Wakkanai.

The morning after our arrival we drove in Half-Safe the few miles to the American outpost and announced ourselves. The Post Commander not only invited us in, but insisted we put up with him in his home and make the post our headquarters for as long as we were in Wakkanai.

Lowell shared a two bedroom house with his second in command and a third of officer who was in charge of a sub-unit attached to the post. Two extra bunks were brought into the bedroom being used by the junior officers, and Carlin and I made ourselves at home.

In addition to making us his house guests, Lowell also extended to us all the privileges of the post, including the mess hall. This was an especially welcome relief after more than two weeks of rice and noodles.

Our first evening on the post, our officer hosts gave an impromptu party in our honor. The only thing I remember about the party is that Carlin and one of the officers had a loud difference of opinion about women, religions and politics, in that order, and instead of going to bed on his bunk when the party ended, Carlin went to sleep on the hardwood floor, insisting it was the only decent bed when a man was drunk.

The next few days were spent checking the jeep out, touching it up here and there with salt-water resistant paint, and stocking it with the food and water we would need during the weeks we would be at sea.

One afternoon a representative of the Wakkanai grade school system telephoned the post and asked if Carlin and I would appear at the school auditorium for the benefit of the children. Since Carlin would have had to speak through me as an interpreter anyway, he suggested I go alone.

I expected a small informal gathering of students, but there were several hundred in a tremendous auditorium lined up row after row. It was agreed that I should confine myself to a brief introduction and then answer questions from the young audience. After a few minutes of initial shyness, response became lively and members of the faculty finally had to asked the students to limit their questions.

The kids wanted to know everything from whether or not Carlin and I had wives, to whether the jeep used American or Japanese gas. After nearly two hours, the principal of the school had to cut the meeting off because it was time for the children to go home.

In the meantime, the fuel tank Carlin had constructed in Kawasaki arrived in Wakkanai by ship. We went to the depot to inspect the tank and make sure that gasoline had been made ready in large drums for the trip to the docks.

Getting Underway the 1st Time

Approximately one week after we arrived in Wakkanai, our preparations were completed. Since there was no beach in the vicinity from which we could drive into the ocean, Carlin made arrangements with the Post Commander for a crane truck to lift the jeep off the dock and set it in the water.

With the portable crane in the lead, our hosts and other interested persons following the truck, and Carlin and I in Half-Safe bringing up the rear, we left the post in a caravan headed for the Wakkanai city docks.

About two miles from the post I noticed water coming out of the exhaust pipe in a steady spray of large droplets. I yelled the information down to Carlin. He pulled the jeep off to one side of the highway and stopped so abruptly I nearly fell off the top.

A vital gasket had busted. It would have been ruinous to run the jeep in that condition, so we set there beside the road until part of the caravan came back to see what had happened to us. We asked them to catch up with the truck and have it tow us back to camp. It was nearly an hour before the truck showed up. It had reached the dock-site where we were to go into the water and had been waiting for us. We got back to the post just in time for supper.

Getting Underway the 2nd Time

Two days later we set out again. This time we made it to the harbor without mishap. As soon as we had attached the propeller and rudder, the jeep was lowered into the ocean—and immediately began to fill with water. The sling-lines had not yet been removed from the jeep, so lifting it out of the water and depositing it back on the dock was no problem. The leak was discovered to be minor and was soon fixed.

Then for the second time Half-Safe was lowered into the water. Our supply of gas had been brought to the docks in drums aboard a second truck. These were now unloaded and we proceeded to fill the inboard tanks on the jeep, then the tow tank, which had also been launched and moored to a dock-piling near the jeep.

It was a much slower process filling the tow tank because the lead-in hose was small and it required some doing to get all the air bubbles out of the tank.

While we were doing this, a representative from the local Immigration Office came up and, in something of a huff, gravely informed us we could not leave Japan without going through the proper exit procedures. We promised to report to his office as soon as we secured the jeep.

Our departure was set for early that afternoon. As the time approached, the dockside began to fill up with people from the American military post, along with several hundred others from the city. There were no speeches or flowers, but there was a lot hand-shaking and picture-taking.

Lowering Half-Safe into the ocean at Wakkanai. I and a helper are positioned to keep the jeep from banging into the stone wall by pushing on it with our feet.

For the benefit of the many cameramen, Carlin shook hands a second time with some of the leading dignitaries then dramatically leaped aboard the jeep.

In doing so, he cracked a section of the cabin roof. The departure was off again. Neither Carlin nor I wanted to go back to the U.S. post a second time and face the curious stares of our hosts of the past several days, so we elected to stay aboard Half-Safe until this new injury was repaired.

There were many among our send-off party who had been skeptical of the expedition and some had predicted we would never get our of the harbor. They must have felt pretty self-satisfied at that moment.

Fortunately, the damage resulting from Carlin's ceremonial leap was slight. The crack was soon patched with a piece of holoplast and sealed tight with rubber paint.

That night I slept inside the jeep and Carlin bedded down on top. It was cold enough that with a sweat shirt, a flannel shirt, two thick wool sweaters, and a jacket on, not to mention two blankets, I woke up chilled several times during the night.

Carlin, on the outside and with less clothing and cover than I, said he slept like a baby.

By noon the next day Half-Safe was once again ship-shape, and the same crowd we had disappointed the day before began collecting on the dock. This time Carlin came aboard as light-footed as a ballet dance. But we were not to get away as easy as that.

In order to get some footage of our departure on his own 16mm camera, Carlin announced we would simulate a take off. The Commander of the Post would shoot the scene with Carlin's camera. Then we would circle around, retrieve the camera and take genuine leave.

That sounded simple enough but it turned out to be a near disaster for both Half-Safe and me. The problem was the torpedo-like fuel tank we were to pull behind us on a nylon rope some 150 feet long. Except for not being loaded with dynamite and a percussion cap, the tank was just as dangerous to us as a torpedo because both ends came to sharp conical points. When the jeep was not moving, the weight of the wet nylon towing rope was enough to start the tank moving in toward us like a slow-motion torpedo.

But the tank didn't need speed. Once it got up any momentum at all, its tremendous weight gave it enough force to stove us in. A further problem was the tank followed in the wake of the jeep only when the jeep was going dead ahead in calm or fairly calm waters.

When Half-Safe changed course, the tank tended to hold the old course until the pressure on the tow rope, now being applied from a different angle, built up to where it literally jerked the tank onto the new course.

This had the effect of increasing the speed of the tank in relation to that of the jeep. If the speed of the tank happened to be increased just after a change in course, there was the danger of it catching up with the jeep and ramming us in the side.

It would have been especially dangerous to turn the jeep in a small circle with the tank at the end of its tow rope.

To avoid these problems, I had been appointed captain of the tank with full responsibility for keeping it away from us any time the jeep was not in motion or we were going through some complicated maneuver for any reason.

While tied up at dockside, the tank was moored by both ends away from the jeep so it couldn't make contact with Half-Safe's fragile skin.

When we were all set to begin the mock run, Carlin instructed me to stand on the fantail (rear end) of the jeep and hold most of the tow line in my hands, letting it out gradually as we got away from the dock. Then when we got out to where we were to make a circle and come back in, I was to take up all but a few yards of the line by pulling the tank in close to us.

This meant good timing and fine coordination between my pulling the tank in and Carlin keeping the jeep in motion and helping me avoid a collision.

Finally, the big moment arrived. We grinned like idiots and waved furiously at the cameras. Then Carlin dropped through the hatchway. I braced myself to keep the pull of the ponderous tank from jerking me into the water when the Half-Safe started up. Much to my relief, Carlin started off slowly, but then he began accelerating rapidly. All at once the drag on the line was so heavy I expected to loose my precarious leg-hold on the back of the jeep and go flying into the water head first. The slack in the tow line sizzled through my hands.

A hundred or so feet before we passed the end of the dock and reached open water, the line snapped taut like a bow-string, sending a shiver through the body of the jeep and slowing it down. Only the tremendous amount of elasticity in the nylon rope, cushioning the shock as it did, prevented a serious mishap.

The tank, now flying through the water like an enraged porpoise, missed the dock pilings by a few feet, and my heart started beating again. We kept going straight for several hundred yards, then Carlin slowed the jeep down—the signal for me to start hauling in the tank.

Because of my own excitement, and because I took it for granted the tank should be pulled in a swiftly as possible, I set to with all my strength. By the time the great yellow monster was in where we wanted it, I was nearly prostrate from exhausttion.

Moving much slower, we re-entered the harbor area behind the dock, and Carlin began maneuvering Half-Safe alongside the pier from which we had started. This made a short, sharp turn necessary. I saw too late that the tank still had too much line. By the time Carlin had completed his half-circle and was edging the jeep up to the dock, the tank was shooting in at us on a 45-degree angle, completely out of control.

There was only one way to stop it from ramming us. That was to block it bodily and attempt to divert its course. At the very last second I swung the lower part of my body down into the water, let the sloping nose of the tank strike me a glancing blow, and at the same time pushed outward against the jeep with my legs and left arm. The measure worked, but only barely.

The steel ring in the nose of the tank came within a fraction of an inch of touching the Half-Safe's thin, protective covering. Carlin was looking out of the hatchway by this time and had seen my desperate action.

"Good boy!" he yelled.

I didn't really appreciate the compliment. It sounded too perfunctory. The run-in with the tank had bruised my side and right leg, and I was still gasping for breath.

"How about going out again?" Carlin's volunteer cameraman shouted. "You went too fast that time!"

Carlin was obviously used to that sort of thing, and immediately disappeared into the cabin. Off we went again. But this time Carlin held the speed down, and I was able to play the tow line out a bit more successfully. I intended to make sure there would be no accidents on that trip.

When Carlin slowed down for me to pull the fuel tank in, I pulled it up to within a few feet of the rear of the jeep, then took several turns with the rope around the spare tire clamped on the back of the cabin so I wouldn't have to withstand the drag of the tank while going back to the dock.

This way the tank was so close to us it couldn't get up much speed on its own, and had a much smaller yawing radius. It also gave me an opportunity to rest.

We made it to the dockside this time without incident, and fortunately so, because we were asked to repeat the same routine once more. When we got back the third time, my whole body was trembling from over-exertion, and I was seeing spots before my eyes. But I wasn't done yet. I still had to hold the tank in and then let it out slowly for our actual departure.

When this was done, it was all I could do to crawl up on top of the jeep and wave feebly at the crowd seeing us off.

After resting on top of the jeep for several minutes, I lowered myself through the hatchway and dropped into the seat beside Carlin. He looked over at me, smiled and winked as if to say "Well, this is the it at last. We're on our way."

I remember this vividly because such demonstrations of camaraderie between us had been rare, and were to be rarer still.

Underway And Out Of Contact

Half an hour later my stomach still felt like it was a balloon full of butterflies. We had had no lunch, and Carlin now suggested I eat something. I stood up, removed the seat on which I had been sitting, reached into the compartment beneath it and took out the first can I touched.

This turned out to be white-bait (minnows). I opened it and began wolfing it down.

"You'd better eat something else with that," Carlin advised.

"This will do fine," I said.

Five minutes after I had scraped the last spoonful out of the can, my stomach felt even more queasy than before. I stood up in the seat with my head and shoulders protruding out of the cabin. I hoped the cool air would make me feel better. It didn't.

A few minutes later the white-bait came up with such force, some of it shot out through my nose. Since we had traveled only a mile or so from our starting point, my un-seaman-like behavior must have been clearly visible to all of our well-wishers who were still following our progress through binoculars. I didn't care whether I'd been seen or not.

When I had finished spitting out the last bitter dregs and wiping my mouth, I dropped back into the seat. Carlin gave no indication he had seen me get sick.

Some time later as we neared Soya Strait, which separates Hokkaido from Russian territory, several ships from the Japanese Coast Guard fell in line with our course and, at a distance of five hundred yards or so, steamed on ahead of us. I had heard before our departure they were going to provide us with an escort until we were past a certain large rock in the center of the Straits, from which the Soviets were said to measure their off-shore rights.

When we reached this point some of the ships sounded their fog horns as a farewell to us. Then all the ships rapidly dropped behind and were lost to our sight. We were on our own.

Before this time I had speculated that on such a small craft the vastness of the sea and the danger inherent in every wave would be a frightening and perhaps overwhelming thing that might sap what little courage I felt I had. But at this point there were no such thoughts in my mind. After a while I decided it must be because riding so low in the water as we did and having such a limited horizon, I couldn't see enough of the ocean to be intimidated by it.

This theory was, I think, borne out in the weeks to come. For while we were inside the jeep our range of vision was only a few hundred yards when the sea was calm, and only a few feet when it was wild. We could see for a number of miles when on top of the jeep during good weather, but at such times the sea was not threatening. As soon as the waves rose to a height of three or four feet, our visibility was reduced to a few feet more than fifty percent of the time.

Another thing also helped to give me a sense of security during even the roughest days. The jeep was bottom-heavy and we literally rode through waves instead of over them. We were bounced around the most by short, choppy waves. The long, broad waves that rose and fell like miniature mountains made it feel like we were on a see-saw, and just gave us an interesting ride.

Living in a Coma

As dusk approached that first night, we had made all of fifteen miles. And now was to begin a routine that was to continue day and night, until I lost all track of time. Looking back now, I can recall only events, sometimes lasting for a few seconds and sometimes for several hours, which were serious enough to constitute an emergency or unusual enough to shock us out of a semi-coma state.

The routine was simple. Carlin and I took turns at steering the jeep; two hours on and two hours off, day and night. The only time the jeep was ever deliberately stopped was for a few minutes each evening to put oil in the engine and, for the first three nights, to use the radio.

As the master mechanic and navigator, Carlin had other duties besides steering, so every second or third watch I would stay at the tiller beyond the two-hour period while he went about plotting our course or doing some other necessary thing.

We got into the habit of eating between every other watch, or every four hours. This meant we ate six times during each twenty-four hour period.

For a while both of us heated whatever canned goods we ate by putting them on the manifold of the engine. As the voyage wore on, I stopped bothering with this and ate everything cold. For a urinal we used a large tin can which was kept on the floor of the jeep next to the right-hand seat. When we wanted to urinate we stood up in the seat, used the can, dumped the urine into the sea, then rinsed the can out by leaning over and catching water in it as we passed through a wave.

Our commode was the wide ocean. When the urge came, we made our way to the back of the jeep, squatted down on the narrow ledge formed by an extra gas tank, and held onto the straps holding the spare tire to the jeep. When the sea was running—which it usually was even on the best days—this narrow perch was often under water. So we took off our socks, trousers and shorts before leaving the cabin.

Whenever the rear end of the jeep went down, as the rear end of ships do, it was necessary to raise our end to keep it from slapping into the ocean. On a number of occasions my timing was off and I became intimate with the cold waters of the Sea of Okhotsk.

After we had been at sea for a number of days, we hit a period of bad weather and it got colder and colder. It was impossible to squat on the ledge without getting wet—sometimes up to the waist. On one particularly bad day, I tried squatting on the lower rim of the spare tire, which was strapped against the sloping back of the jeep at a 45 degree angle. I found that by squatting only part of the way, I could miss fouling the ledge and also avoid getting my rear dunked into the ocean each time the jeep plunged into the water.

From this stage it was only a short step to the discovery that I could leave my trousers on and just drop them down as one normally does. I count this development as one of the highlights of the trip.

The tedium of two hours up and perhaps an hour and a half in a short, uncomfortable bunk is in itself enough to wear one out. The exhausting effort required to keep the jeep on course, plus the constant droning of the engine in the restricted cabin and the motion of the jeep, had reduced us to a semi-coma state by the end of the third day. Just thinking was a difficult exercise.

We lost all desire to talk and sometimes went for days with hardly a word to each other. We steered, ate, took care of our bodily needs, then crawled into the narrow bunk space behind the seats and sank gratefully into unconsciousness.

The Yellow Monster

Carlin had arranged for us to make radio contact with a station in Wakkanai each evening. In order to use the radio, the jeep had to be stopped and the engine cut off. This meant the tank behind us was then turned into a veritable bomb tethered at the end of a rope which by itself was enough to pull the tank in on us. But even more serious was the wind and the action of the waves. We could never tell from which direction the tank was going to come.

When Carlin was on the radio I had two duties: keep the outside radio antenna dry by wiping it with a cloth, and keep the tank away from the jeep.

I quickly found out either one of these jobs was enough to keep me busy full time. The first evening the sea wasn't too rough, but there was a thick fog. This made it necessary to wipe the antenna every twenty or thirty seconds. About five minutes after we stopped, the tank found our range and began boring in on us. There was absolutely nothing I could do until it got within reach.

The skin of the fuel tank was relatively thick, but not so thick as to be treated carelessly. The slightest puncture from a sharp jab would have been a major disaster—probably our last. So Carlin had constructed tiny reinforced metal eyelets at each end of the tank, and one on each side at the center.

As an instrument to catch the tank and shove it away when it approached the jeep, we had a grappling hook which measured some ten feet in length. The wood shaft of this hook was about two inches in diameter. On one end of the shaft was a combination hook and punch made of steel. Altogether the hook weighed some seven or eight pounds.

The two end and two center eyelets on the tank, each about the size of a silver dollar, were the only spots where it could be touched with the boat hook. Therefore, whenever the tank began to threaten the jeep it was necessary to first snag one of these little rings with the steel tipped hook and then shove or otherwise maneuver the tank away.

The closer the tank got to us the more dangerous it became, so it was important to stop it as soon as it could be reached with the hook. This meant it was necessary to grasp the boat hook at the end and extend it out from the body with the arms. The weight of the hook itself made this an awkward and tiring position. But there were worse factors.

Swinging free on a rope 150 feet long, the tank could come in at us from any direction when we were drifting. If it approached us from the front I, had to clamber down off the cabin to the jeep's tiny prow and meet it there. If it came in from the rear, that is where I had to be. The sides of the jeep were the most vulnerable of all because the height of the cabin above the water allowed the tank to get about four feet closer to us before I could reach it with the boat hook.

Now comes the interesting part. The bow of the jeep was about the size of a small desk, one end of which tapered to a point. This area was cluttered with various fixtures. The top of the cabin measured about five by seven feet. About one-fourth of this space was taken up by large wicker baskets in which emergency gear was stored. The hatchway took up some more space, and there were a number of other things like an air vent, guide-lines and the exhaust pipe that kept the top from being as open and smooth as a football field. The small, flat ledge across the back of the jeep extended out about ten inches.

This was the total area of the top of the jeep, and the platform from which I had to operate to fight off the tank— usually on my knees and often on my stomach.

Even during the best weather there was always enough wind and wave action to make Half-Safe bob and weave. My own weight when I moved from one side to the other would tilt it. As a result, it was dangerous to stand upright on the jeep without holding onto something under any circumstances, much less while holding onto a heavy 10-foot long boat hook and trying at the same time to snare a small ring on a gas-filled tank which was slithering and tossing around in the waves below.

In all of the weeks I spent in and on the jeep at sea, I remember only a couple of occasions, neither of which was long than a few seconds, during which time I stood up without holding on with one hand or being braced in some way.

The worse the weather the worse the tank behaved, and the more difficult it was to maneuver on the jeep. Time after time I had to fling myself from one part of the topside to another without regard for where I might fall. If my legs had not been protected by thick trousers, I hate to imagine the damaged they would have suffered. As it was, the bumps and bruises sustained during some of the worst periods stayed with me for weeks.

After trying that first evening for over half an hour to make radio contact with Wakkanai, Carlin gave up. Our radio would receive but he couldn't send. The implications of this hardly affected me at all. In a way I was glad because it meant we would get underway again, freeing me from the monster tied to our tail. If Carlin was tempted to turn around and go back because of the failure of the radio, he gave no indication of it to me.

"To hell with the bloody thing!" he said. "We'll try it again tomorrow when it shouldn't be so wet outside."

The second evening was not as foggy but still the radio wouldn't work. After fussing with it for close to an hour, Carlin again gave up. Following the third attempt he gave up all together.

The next few days passed without serious incident. Day by day the weather grew colder, and to keep warm we began running with the hatch-cover closed. Some time after this both Carlin and I came down with splitting headaches. With the cover down the cabin had filled with carbon monoxide. We jammed the door so it wouldn't close all the way, and opened a narrow vent in the rear window.

Our headaches disappeared. Closing the hatch even part way, however, produced another problem. Without the free circulation of air through the cabin moisture begin to condense on the inside. We first noticed this when lying in the bunk. Water started dripping off the ceiling into our faces.

We thought the ceiling was leaking where it had been cracked during the boarding incident. But the whole interior of the jeep soon became steeped in water, the walls and ceiling dripping like so many bad faucets.

In no time, the bunk and all our bedding was fairly well soaked. We tried covering the bunk with a life jacket. I put a second life jacket over my head when I went to sleep to keep the water off my face.

The Kurile Islands

Shortly after beginning our second week at sea, Carlin announced that we should soon be able to sight the Kurile Islands. Our course called for us to pass through the Russian-held chain just south of the small island of Makanru-to.

The islands were reportedly inhabited by Russian fishermen, and there were Soviet coast guard patrols in the area.

"If we meet anyone, act friendly," Carlin advised in all seriousness.

About mid-morning, and within an hour of the time predicted by Carlin, the snow-capped peaks of one of the larger islands floated up over the horizon. A short while later, Makanru-to shimmered into view. We set our course dead for the island.

Some five hours later we could see the surf pounding rocks off the southwest corner of the little island. We altered our course slightly to bring us up to the southern and leeward side. At that point, the wind was whipping the water around us into white caps and we were bouncing over short, choppy waves.

As soon as we entered the lee side of the island, the waves flattened out as if someone had laid a piece of glass over them. The weather had not really been very bad so far, but this was the first smooth water we had encountered. We were now within less than a mile of the shore. Carlin couldn't locate any signs of habitation on the beach, and decided to go in close.

The surface of the sea was now glassier than ever. There was no wind to speak of and the sun was warm. Except for a certain grimy feeling that came from sleeping in the same salt-caked clothing for more than a week, the peculiar deadening affects of the endlessly roaring engine and our unnatural sleeping schedule, we could have been weekend sailing on an indoor lake.

When we were about three hundred yards out from the shore, the clear depths of the water were suddenly obscured by a dark undulating cloud-mass which seemed to breathe with the movement of the sea. The closer we got to the shore, the nearer the surface floated this mysterious submarine cloud. Finally when it was not more than a few feet below us we discovered what it was: a giant forest of alaria—the famous winged kelp of the North Pacific, growing like huge vines from depths of well over 100 feet.

The way the giant kelp streamers were "flying" westward a few feet below the surface was evidence the water was flowing steadily in that direction.

The kelp forest ended about seventy-five feet from shore. We could see the bottom then, and I estimated the water to be six to ten feet deep. Carlin cut the Half-Safe's engine and we drifted to a stop in a little pocket where the water was dead calm. I tried to reach bottom with the boat hook. Then I dropped a can overboard.

It planed down at a steep angle, growing smaller and smaller. When it finally came to rest on the bright sandy bottom, I revised my estimate of the depth of the water to fifty feet.

Instead of a beach, Makanru-to was ringed with a skirt of bleached driftwood—great trees, logs and cut lumber, piled up many feet thick and extending for fifteen yards or more up the steep, rocky shoreline. The uppermost part of this tremendous wooden girdle was probably thirty feet above sea-level.

Beyond the driftwood, directly in front of us, was a small slide sloping up sharply to a promontory rising to perhaps 300 feet. The slide was spotted with a scraggily coat of grass, and there were bright-colored flowers here and there in the raw earth.

Our view to the west ended a few hundred yards away in a sheer, rock wall. Looking eastward, we could see there was a plain rising gradually from the beach.

The only sign of life was a few birds flying around the cliff to the west of us. Their cries came to us faintly, as if out of a dream.

There was nothing to fear except loneliness itself. But we had not been there more than ten minutes before the awfulness of nothing began to make itself felt. The ghost-white of the bleached wood, the distant cries of birds, the soft eternal slapping of the water against the sides of the jeep, formed in my mind a picture of intimate loneliness so intense I wanted to cry out as if this blind action would awaken the dead little world surrounding us and put life into it.

After a while, Carlin went ashore by jumping from Half-Safe onto the driftwood. He walked around for a few minutes and then came back aboard. While he was ashore, I sat on the jeep wondering how long the driftwood would burn if it were set afire.

Then for the first time we transferred gas from the tow tank behind us into one of the inboard tanks. The procedure was simple. And there in the calm of the lee, easy to accomplish. We drew the tank up next to the prow of the jeep, and attached tiny transparent polyethylene hoses to two nipples on the tank—one to carry gasoline out of it. A hand operated bicycle pump was used to force air into the fuel tank. Because of the small diameter of the hoses, however, it took more than an hour to transfer the amount of gas wanted.

Afterward, Carlin turned on the radio set and we took turns listening to ham operators in Australia and Japan, and to what appeared to be broadcasts from Radio Moscow. Later we rested. Before getting underway, Carlin made a special point of brushing his teeth. I didn't bother.

Our next leg was to take us across a remote corner of the North Pacific, and there would be no more land until we reached the Aleutian Islands. When Carlin started the jeep's engine and we began to move through the water at our usual turtle's pace, the idea of how very small and presumptuous we were suddenly flooded my mind and made me uneasy for the first time.

I knew this thought had occurred because for the first time since leaving Wakkanai, there was something with which to compare our size and speed—in this case the tiny island of Makanru.

Once out of sight of land the constant motion of the water made it possible to imagine we were traveling much faster than our true speed, and so gave the impression we were making rapid progress toward a goal. But just let the Half-Safe's engine stop or even falter like it was going to stop, and this reassuring feeling disappeared like a mirage.

The sudden quiet that followed was like waking up from a pleasant dream and finding one's self in a real-life nightmare—drifting helplessly on a small piece of metal and pressed wood hundreds of miles at sea without any means of contacting the outside world.

There is no way to express the feeling of relief that engulfed me every time the jeep engine caught again after a stop, and began its steady roar.

Trapped in a Kelp Field

The swift-flowing current that had kept the long kelp branches beneath the surface while we were approaching the island had begun to reverse its direction, and as soon as we crossed the narrow kelp-free belt we found ourselves slowed to a crawl. The kelp had risen to the surface. The clogged water seemed to have the consistency of jelly.

We continued to force our way through the kelp-covered sea for several minutes. Then we hit an exceptionally thick patch and the Half-Safe shuddered to a stop, choking the engine out. The propeller had been fouled.

It took about fifteen minutes to cut the kelp away from the propeller and drive shaft—by leaning over from the rear-end ledge and reaching under the jeep. Then we began to move forward again, cautiously threading our way between the heavier patches and traveling parallel with the long streamers.

I stood on the prow of the jeep doing what I could to clear a path for us with the boat hook. Just as we were passing out of the kelp field, there was a shocking loud whack from the rear of the jeep and the engine stopped dead. Carlin came out of the hatchway as if he had been fired from a cannon, and practically flew to the back of the jeep.

I followed him. A rope had been left trailing off the back of Half-Safe and had become caught in the propeller, jamming the drive shaft as tight as if it had been welded.

Carlin' s fear was that the shaft might have been bent or twisted by the impact. If that happened, we were out of business. Within a few seconds, Carlin had stripped off his clothes and let himself down into the cold water. It took him about half an hour to cut the main part of the rope away from the propeller and shaft.

Part of the rope had been shredded to strands and pulled into the cutless bearing. There was no way to get them out without dismantling the drive shaft—something that was out of the question while the jeep was in the water.

Finally, Carlin decided to start the engine and then gradually engage the propeller to see if he could break it loose that way. The first attempt was unsuccessful. Then using a wrench, he managed to turn the propeller shaft a little by hand. This apparently broke it loose, for the next time he engaged the propeller shaft it groaned, squeaked and then began to turn.

After a few minutes test, the shaft and propeller seemed to be working all right. Carlin put his clothes back on. We headed the jeep away from the island and were off.

Into the North Pacific

It was a windy but clear day. We could see the Kuriles behind us for hour after hour. They were still there on the horizon, as faint grey smudges, when the sun went down that night.

Everything went well for the next couple of days. There was a constant, cold wind. But the sky was bright and the sea was an icy blue decorated with brilliant white caps that gave it a picture-postcard look. The nights began to grow perceptibly shorter and the water got colder. We expected to see ice in it at any time.

Visitors from Russia

About three days after we left the Kuriles we thought we were going to have visitors. A large ship came over the horizon off to our left. After a little while it changed course and began bearing down on us. I was at the tiller, and Carlin went top-side.

When the ship was a few hundred yards off our port side, it changed course again to pass us going in the opposite direction. Carlin came below.

"Is it Russian?" I asked.

"Yes. Go on up and take a look," he said.

As I hoisted myself through the hatchway, Carlin yelled: "Wave at them...and smile!"

I saw no activity on the ship. There was nobody in sight. This would have been enough to confirm it as a Russian vessel even if the Soviet flag had not been visible on the smoke-stack. If it had been any other nationality, the railing would have been lined with curious sailors staring bug-eyed at the strange apparition bobbing around in the water below them.

The ship maintained its new course and soon disappeared over our limited horizon.

Early in the morning about two days after this, we sighted a number of fishing vessels on the horizon. They appeared to be on a course that would bring them near us, and we began looking forward to our first contact since leaving Japan. Carlin told me to go top-side and engage them in conversation as soon as they came near enough. He wanted to check our location with them.

I got ready but no sooner had I climbed out on the cabin than the ships abruptly changed course and scooted away from us like a flock of disturbed ducks. They were Japanese ships.

"Now what caused that?" I shouted down to Carlin.

"Beats me," he said. "They acted like something scared them off."

A few hours later we spied another ship lying directly ahead of us and only a mile or so away. This ship was just barely moving. As we got closer we discovered why. Crewmen were pulling a net in. When we were near enough to discern the actions of individual members of the crew, there appeared to be some excitement on the ship. But by the time we got within hailing distance the disturbance had apparently died down.

It turned out that when they first saw us they thought we were a Russian submarine, and had been debating about cutting their net and fleeing. I related our experience with the ships earlier that morning, and found they had heard about the incident over their radio.

The Japanese crew members told us they had been at sea for two months. They had also heard about our departure from Wakkanai via radio. They were mystified by how we could travel so far from Hokkaido with no more fuel than what could have been carried in the jeep.

They had not heard about the fuel tank. When I pointed it our to them they wanted to know how we got gas from the tank into the jeep.

We shouted back and forth to each other for about fifteen minutes. When we started on our way the ship's crew asked us if there was anything we needed. When I shook my head "No" one of the crew held up a large fish he had just gutted, and pantomimed, "Not even this fish?"

We laughed and left them shaking their heads in wonder. Our meeting with the boat had been a pleasant interlude, but it lasted for only a few minutes and was soon forgotten. We continued on, the sea a white-frosted shimmering blue.

Gassing Up in Rough Weather

Transferring gas from the tank into the jeep had posed no problem the first time it was done because we had been in the lee of Makanru-to where there were no waves or wind. I dreaded the day when we would have to make the transfer in the open sea. I knew we would have trouble even in the calmest weather.

On about our seventh day out from the Kuriles, Carlin announced that if the weather permitted, we would attempt a transfer on the following day.

There was a blustery cold wind blowing the next day and the waves continued to crest at five to eight feet hour after hour. By mid-afternoon it appeared unlikely that there was going to be any appreciable change during the few hours of light remaining, and the attempt was put off until the next day.

The postponement brought a great sense of relief to me, although I knew the following day might be worse and, as Carlin pointed out, we would have no choice then.

That night the wind rose higher, pushing the water into waves that, from our low vantage point, looked like small hills. The next morning the wind was still blowing, but in such a way as to break the waves up and fill the air with spray. It was overcast and cold.

As the day wore on, the sky cleared a little and it warmed up a bit. I had been steeling myself since dawn for the ordeal I knew was coming. But when Carlin gave the command to cut the engine, it was still something of a shock.

Within minutes after the jeep stopped, a dirty grey overcast blotted out the already weak sun and the wind picked up speed, dropping the temperature several degrees. While Carlin prepared the transfer hoses, stripped up to the waist and got ready to launch himself in our one-man rubber life-raft, I went aft to work the tank around to the front of the jeep. By now the sea was a slate grey and the waves had lengthened out into rolling swells. From the amount of spray in the air, it might as well have been raining.

Thinking to make it easier to herd the gas tank to the bow-end of the jeep, I began pulling it up to the rear with the idea of "walking" it along the side instead of prodding it along with the boat hook.

In the meantime, Carlin had inflated the tiny raft, boarded it, and was now hanging onto a rope he had attached to the jeep to keep himself from being blown away. He was using the life-raft because it would be easier to fasten the transfer hoses to the far end of the tank from the raft, since he would be able to pull himself right up to the tank and then have both hands free for the job. Otherwise he would have to hold onto the jeep with both feet and one hand, and at the same time contend with a tank that was weaving and bobbing in a rhythm invariably the reverse of the jeep's movements.

Carlin was ready before I got the tank in position. I had pulled it to within twenty feet of the rear of the jeep when he began yelling. I had on a knitted sock cap pulled down over my ears to ward off the cold wind, and couldn't hear him clearly.

"What did you say?" I yelled back to him.

He yelled again but I still couldn't understand what he said. From the tone of his voice, however, it was easy to tell he was on the verge of another explosion. I stopped pulling on the tow rope and raised my ear flaps so I could hear better.

'Take that god-damned cap off!" he screamed.

But now that I could hear there was no reason to take the cap off.

"I will not!" I yelled back.

"Take it off before I knock it off!" he thundered.

"Go ahead and try it!" I challenged.

He mimicked me in a whining voice, screwing up his face like some kind of an idiot. Then he yelled again.

"I thought I told you to bring that tank around here!"

"That's what I'm doing," I answered. "I'm shortening the line to make it easier to handle."

"Let it out! Let it out!" he screamed, repeating himself.

I tossed the line I had gathered into my hands back into the water. Almost instantly the tank scooted back about twenty-five yards.

"Now what are you doing?" Carlin shouted.

"I let it out!" I yelled back.

Carlin's voice quivered with intense rage. "You fucking idiot! Oh! You fucking idiot!" He began paddling toward the rear of the jeep, mumbling and cursing.

There was no possible way of getting the tank around where it was wanted without pulling it most of the way in, so I picked up the tow line and once again began hauling it in. This time, fortunately, the tank began to drift around toward the front by itself and met Carlin at about the half-way mark. Between us we finally managed to get it into position lying at a right angle to the jeep with about three feet separating the nose of the tank from the jeep.

We passed a line from the jeep through the nose ring of the tank to prevent it from getting too far away from us. Carlin attached the air and gas hoses to the tank nipples. He had allowed for considerable play in the hoses so the constant movement of the tank and jeep wouldn't break the connections.

It was my duty to man the air pump which forced gas out of the tank into Half-Safe. At the same time, I had to prevent the tank from battering us to pieces.

As soon as the hoses were in place, I began pumping. Carlin re-boarded the jeep and busied himself in the cabin. I had rolled my trouser legs up above my knees, because every minute or so a wave broke over the bow of the jeep and sloshed onto my feet and legs.

Now it began to rain in cold, driving sheets. The diameter of the hoses was already miniscule. The continual movement of the tank and jeep further reduced their carrying capacity by keeping them partly pinched off all the time.

Several times I pumped away for as long as ten minutes without any gas passing into the jeep because one or the other of the hoses was completely closed off. After about an hour the sky had grown lead black, and nearly every wave broke over the tiny deck of the jeep, sometimes swirling up above my knees. I moved back as far as the length of the hoses would allow, and climbed up on the forward slope of the cabin. This kept the icy water off my legs most of the time.

Every few minutes I had to scramble back down onto the prow and shove the fuel tank back out to the end of its leash. I cannot recall how much longer I clung to the guide-lines of the bucking jeep, pumping away until one arm was numb then switching to the other.

A long time after I told myself I couldn't keep it up any longer, Carlin appeared on top of the jeep.

"It's getting too rough! Let's call it quits!" he yelled.

By the time we got the hose lines disengaged from the tank, some of the waves breaking over the prow were nearly waist deep. When I saw a big one coming, I would stop whatever I was doing and clamber up on the cabin until it passed. The rain had continued all the time and was getting heavier. It took about fifteen minutes to free the tank, and prod it out where the wind would catch it and swing it off to the side.

We then secured the deck and got underway. Because I was wet and cold, Carlin volunteered to take my turn at the tiller. I wrung some water out of my trousers without taking them off, and crawled into the bunk.

The First Collision

About an hour before dawn some two days after making the gas transfer, the tranquil period that had followed came to an abrupt and loud end. Carlin was at the tiller and I was asleep in the bunk behind him. There was a sudden, tremendous thud from the bottom of the jeep. At the same instant the engine died, and we stopped as if we had hit something. The noise shocked me awake and I was out of the bunk before I knew it.

The eerie silence that always followed the cutting of the engine had already set in and my voice sounded hollow and un-real.

"What happened?" I asked automatically.

Carlin didn't answer. He didn't have to. The sudden explosive sound had been exactly the same as the one when the propeller had fouled on the dragging rope back at Makanru-to.

But how? There was no possible way a second rope could have fallen overboard. We had made certain of that. What was there in mid-ocean we could run into? Already on the side of the jeep beneath the cabin exit, I scrambled out, closely followed by Carlin. It was still dark.

We could see nothing. Yet the jeep was stuck fast. In a moment the wind and the movement of the waves swung the jeep to one side, indicating that whatever held us fast was caught somewhere on the rear of the jeep. There was nothing we could do but wait for the coming dawn. So there we sat, swinging in a small arc, in the grip of something we couldn't see or identify.

Because the high wind was cold and the spray heavy, we sat in the cabin waiting for daylight. Luckily we were released for once from having to keep a constant vigil on the tank behind us because the wind kept it at a safe distance, rearing and plunging like a sea serpent caught on a line.

As the grey-black of the horizon was suffused with pale light, we began trying to peer through the cloak of darkness that still covered the sea around us. At first we could see nothing. The wind had abated somewhat but the ocean continued to writhe in dark, ominous swells, only vaguely discernible.

To me the sea then seemed most like a creature alive; the swells rising and falling like giant lungs, the oily surface glistening like the back of a gargantuan whale. This condition lasted for about ten minutes. Then in a matter of seconds the sea changed from black to grey-white and began to sparkle brightly.

A moment later the mystery was solved. Several hundred feet away from the jeep we saw a small red pennant floating on top of a slender staff embedded in a tiny buoy. We had fouled a submerged fishing net and been caught like any other fish.

We couldn't see them but we knew that strung out on both sides of us at intervals of a few hundred feet was a regular fence of the small pennants, marking the location of a net that was probably a mile or more long. We had apparently hit the net somewhere in between two pennants.

But it would not have made any difference if we had approached a pennant dead-on. If we had been running with lights, and for some reason Carlin had been looking ahead instead of at the compasses, our momentum would still have carried us into the net even if he had spotted it.

The only possible preventive measure if we had been on the lookout for a pennant in the first place would have been to cut the engine the instant the flag was seen. Then at least the prop would not have been seriously fouled.

At that point, conjecture and hindsight provided little consolation. We had fouled the prop a second time—and possibly damaged it beyond repair.

As soon as we discovered what had happened, we took the boat hook and began groping along the side of the jeep, finally snagging the top of the net. To prevent the net from ripping all the way in two when we began sawing it away from the prop, Carlin cut the top strand-rope and tied the ends to the sides of the jeep. Then kneeling on the back ledge and thrusting his arm into the water up to his shoulder, he sliced, pulled and hacked at the mess shrouding the propeller and drive shaft for about half an hour.

In the meantime, the wind changed several times and I was kept busy battling the tank.

When Carlin had cut away all of the fouled net he could, he started the engine and engaged the propeller drive. For the first few seconds it seemed like the shaft had been jammed tight and wasn't going to move this time. Finally it broke loose and began to revolve. The white froth of water boiling up from behind the jeep was the most beautiful thing I could hope to see. Now satisfied that we were again mobile, we tied the cut ends of the net-rope back together and cast it away from the jeep.

The wind had blown the fuel tank over the net, and we had to circle around it to get back on course. It was some three hours since I had been startled awake by our impact with the net.

Despite the danger we had been in and the fact that he got well soaked in frigid water while cutting away the net, Carlin was in good enough humor to speculate wryly on how the fishermen would react when they found their spliced net later that morning.

We didn't know for sure who had laid the net, but there was very little doubt that it belonged to a ship from the Japanese fleet we had sighted. There was bound to be more than one net in the area, and to avoid another such experience as we had just gone through, we began a constant vigil for the tiny warning flags.

Late that evening, while there was still enough light to see, our watch was rewarded. I was at the tiller and spotted one of the waving flags when we were about fifty feet from it. I yelled out a warning to the sleeping Carlin and at the same time reached up to turn off the ignition switch.

Carlin was out of the bunk before I could flick the switch, however. His hand closed on mine and we both turned off the ignition. Carlin could move fast when he wanted to.

As soon as the engine stopped, the jeep began drifting sideways toward the net. Carlin popped his head out of the hatchway to see if he could spot any other pennants and thereby discover which way the net was running. He found the string of flags almost immediately and dived back into the cabin.

"Start the engine!" he shouted. "We're drifting into the net!"

At the same time that I flicked the ignition and jabbed the starter button, Carlin grabbed the tiller from my hand and jerked it toward him. The engine started instantly and we began moving.

We had drifted sideways from our original course and were now traveling parallel to the net-only a few feet from it. As soon as we picked up speed, the jeep began veering off away from the net and back in the direction from which we had just come.

"Hold it there!" Carlin shouted, signaling for me to take the tiller. Then he returned to the hatchway, stood there about ten seconds surveying the situation and then popped back into the cabin and grabbed the tiller over my hands and altered our course several degrees to the right.

"Hold it there!" he repeated in a shout, and again went back to the hatchway. About thirty seconds later he ducked back into the cabin, holding his left arm bent at the elbow with the forearm sticking out from his body.

"Follow the movements of my hand with the tiller!" he directed. "When I move my hand this way you move the tiller the same say."

He demonstrated what he meant. "Do you understand?" he barked loudly.

I nodded my head and shouted "Yes" much louder than necessary. I resented him implying that things had to be reduced to their simplest terms before I could grasp them. He glared at me then returned to the hatchway, his left hand still in the cabin and pointing about fifteen degrees to the right of the course we were then on. I swung the tiller over to coincide with his signal.

We held this course for several seconds then he moved his hand further to the right.

For the next several minutes we zig-zagged in short spurts as I continued to follow Carlin's hand directions. A wind had come up and was whipping the water into good-sized waves, making it difficult for the jeep to respond to Carlin's rapid course changes. Seconds after giving me a half-right rudder signal he dropped into the cabin doing everything but foaming at the mouth.

"You're running us into the net, you god-damned fool!" he screamed, slamming the tiller full left. His ear was right in my mouth.

"I'm on your course!" I yelled into it.

Grim-faced, Carlin sprang back to the open hatch. I glanced out the small window to my right and saw one of the warning pennants only feet from the jeep. It had to be the last flag marking the end of the net. I cursed Carlin silently for cutting it so close.

Now we were past the net but the fuel tank was not. Being more susceptible to the wind than the jeep, it was being blown right into it. I held my breath and I imagine Carlin did too.

There was a chance the tank would slide over the top of the net without fouling it. When there was no sudden shudder from the tow line and the yellow nose of the tank could still be seen cavorting behind us sixty seconds later, the air came out of me like I'd been punctured. I felt weak all over.

Carlin ducked back into the cabin and closed the hatch cover. Now that we had escaped disaster, his mood changed immediately.

"Good thing you spotted that!" he said in an unusually friendly tone. A short while later he crawled into the bunk and went back to sleep.

The Second Collision

About 2:30 that night, half an hour after I had been relieved at the tiller and gone to sleep, came the same sickening thud from the bottom of the jeep, followed by the same eerie silence that meant a dead engine.

I had spent the previous eight hours praying that if it had to happen again, it would happen during one of Carlin's watches—not mine. I didn't want to be put in a position where he could blame me for something as serious as that. I wasn't a mechanic, but I knew as well as he did that we had pushed our luck already. The propeller shaft wouldn't take much more of that sort of punishment—if any.

When the tell-tale shock came, I said to myself, "Well, your prayers were answered." Even though I was concerned enough about the collision and the terrible possibility we might be permanently disabled, I was glad it hadn't been me at the wheel, and gave silent thanks before struggling out of the bunk. I was so relieved, in fact, it was necessary to exert some effort to prevent myself from smiling.

As it had the first time we hit a net, the jeep was bobbing and swinging in a small arc just as if we were held by an anchor with a short line. This time, however, the wind wasn't in our favor, and the fuel tank began immediately to drift in on us. Both Carlin and I climbed out on top of Half-Safe. The sky was overcast and it was dark. There was a bitter cold, wet wind blowing. We couldn't see anything in the way of warning flags.

"We'll have to wait until daylight," Carlin said. "You finish your break. I'll watch the tank."

We lowered ourselves into the jeep, and I climbed back into the bunk. Carlin sat down in the steersman's seat, leaned up against the side of the cabin and relaxed. Every twenty seconds or so he would look out the window behind him at the tank, which was riding the waves about thirty feet out. In about ten minutes the tank had inched up to where it was no more than five feet from us. It was pitching and plunging wildly in the wind-swept sea.

Carlin scrambled out of the cabin and gave it a shove with the boat hook. The force of his push sent the tank back out to where it had been. He dropped into the cabin and resumed his relaxed position. I dropped off to sleep.

The next thing I recall was a loud whack somewhere near my head, and Carlin struggling to get out of the cabin. The hatch cover made a loud clatter as it slammed into the roof-top. Carlin added to the noise by falling around while tying to get the boat hook loose from its moorings.

I raised up from the bunk and looked out the window to see if I could locate the fuel tank. It was about eighteen inches from my nose, and bucking like a crazed stallion. I though it was going to come through the side of the jeep any second, and jumped out of the bunk.

By that time, Carlin had the boat hook and was jabbing frantically at the tank's nose ring. Finally he caught it and began working the ugly monster back away from the jeep. A moment later Carlin lowered himself into the cabin. He was breathing hard, but was not as agitated as I expected him to be.

Without looking at me or speaking, he crawled over onto the bunk to see how much damage the tank had done. About four or five inches from where my head had been was an ugly bulge in the metal skin of the jeep. It looked as if someone had put a blunt steel punch up against it and hit the punch one tremendous blow.

The skin was not broken, however, and so the bulge didn't constitute either an inconvenience or danger. The tank had barely touched us, apparently when it had raised up on a wave and swung forward as the water dropped. Carlin had either dozed off or failed to check the tank often enough—another near disaster that had happened while he was on duty.

I knew my luck wasn't going to hold forever, and thinking of all the different ways it could end made me apprehensive. It was time for me to begin my watch. I took over and Carlin climbed into the bunk. The tank was kinder to me. I had to go out and shove it away only three or four times in the next two hours.

My watch was up at six. Dawn had already broken by that time and I knew I wasn't going to get any more sleep until we were free from the net—if then.

I intended to let Carlin sleep on, but he awoke on his own accord and got up. He opened the hatch cover and looked around outside. It was still bitter cold.

"This is going to be a chilly job," he said, ducking back into the cabin. He began rummaging around in his gear behind the bunk, pulling out a half gallon bottle of O' sake.

"So the situation calls for a little fortifier," he added. After a long drink, he passed the bottle to me. I helped myself and handed it back to him. For the next thirty minutes he drank steadily. I took one now and then.

Shortly before seven it was as light as it was going to get and the cold wind had subsided a little. Carlin had finished all but about a pint of the O'sake. He was drunk enough to be glassy-eyed and awkward on his feet. He stood up and began removing his clothes.

When he was completely stripped he climbed out on the cabin top, a knife in between his teeth like an island native getting ready to dive after a shark. I followed along behind him. We could see net pennants on both sides of us. We had hit the net in almost the exact center between two flags, where there was nothing to see but dark water.

Shivering from the cold wind, Carlin kneeled down on the back of the jeep, and with me holding onto him so he wouldn't topple into the sea, he began sawing away at the main part of the net entangled around the prop.

A few minutes after he started to work, the ship in whose net we were caught came over the horizon and bore down on us. They had apparently seen us long before I spotted them, and were coming in at full speed. When I told Carlin we were going to have company he grunted and continued to saw away at the jammed net.

He could not reach back under the jeep far enough to get it all. Like a man crawling into his own grave, he lowered himself into the icy water. Naturally fair-skinned, Carlin now had the look of frozen marble.

Holding on to the rear of the jeep with one hand and floating free in the water, he began again cutting away at the net. After about five minutes of this, he started ducking down under the jeep, staying under water as long as he could. While he was doing this, the fishing boat arrived on the scene and approached to within about twenty-five yards. They could see what had happened and didn't ask any silly questions.

Carlin crawled out of the water and sat down on the cross-ledge.

At his direction, I yelled for the ship's crew to lend us some knives. They immediately tied two fish knives to a line and threw them to us. Carlin took one of the knives and went back into the water. Again he began ducking his head and working under water for a minute or so at a time.

The fishermen lining the rail of the ship were afraid Carlin would go into shock from the cold, lose his grip on the jeep and drown. I passed their shouted warnings along to Carlin, but he ignored them. I spent the next five minutes yelling up to the crew members that he would be all right.

They couldn't believe that a man could stay in water that cold as long as Carlin had, and continued to shout at me to make him get out. Carlin had readied his 35mm camera before going into the water the first time, and now instructed me to get it and take pictures of him working on the prop. This really amazed the fishermen.

Finally, Carlin climbed out of the water and, shivering as if he was in his death throes, dragged himself into the cabin of the jeep, wrapped up in blankets and drank some more of the O' sake.

In the meantime, the crew of the fishing ship had launched a small dinghy and one of the crew members, a powerfully built young man in his late teens or early twenties, rowed to the Half-Safe, tied up to us and came aboard. He brought with him another knife lashed to a long staff.

Standing on the rear of the jeep with me he stuck the pole down under Half-Safe and began trying to slash away the net shreds still jamming the prop. He had some success.

I then tried my hand at it. I knew the make-up of the prop and shaft and had more success than he did. But we couldn't see what we were doing, and finally gave up.

A few minutes later, Carlin threw off his blankets, climbed out of the cabin and once again lowered himself into the water. The Japanese fishermen couldn't believe their eyes, and again and again shouted for him to get out of the water before it was too late.

Carlin was now completely drunk but he realized the danger he was exposing himself to and this time rigged a rope around his chest. I held onto the rope while he was in the water. While holding onto the rope, I couldn't keep close watch on the fuel tank.

Just as Carlin came up for air the third time, the tank shot in toward his head. It was within a foot of him before I could get hold of it and shove it away. My push sent the tank off to one side of the jeep, and I momentarily forgot about it. Three or four minutes later I glanced back along-side of the jeep.

It was coming in, riding the waves like a surfboard. Both myself and the young fisherman, who had seen me ward the tank off before, began a mad scramble for the boat hook. The fisherman got to the hook first, hastily swung it over the emergency gear basket in which I had put Carlin's camera and accidentally hooked the carrying strap of the camera.

The camera was sent flying high up into the air and out over the front of the jeep in a wide arc. It plummeted into the ocean twenty or so feet in front of the Half-Safe and sank like a piece of lead.

I knew how Carlin felt about his cameras, and I knew how important they were to him—to say nothing of the fact that the one that had just disappeared into two miles of ocean was worth over four hundred dollars. As soon as we had the tank under control, I returned to the rear of the jeep where Carlin was resting; still in the water.

"Ben, the boy accidentally knocked your camera overboard and it is lost," I told him. I had to repeat this twice before he could understand what I was talking about. When he did understand, he went mad. Already shaking from an experience that would surely have incapacitated if not killed an ordinary man, Carlin now began to tremble with an insane fury. Then he exploded into a string of curses.

"Why didn't you jump in after it? Why didn't you jump in after it?" he screamed over and over.

Then he started cursing again and beating the rear of the jeep with his fist. The fisherman who had knocked the camera over-board came up beside me. He and the other crew members of the fishing boat, who were watching the scene from the deck of their ship, had been convinced before that Carlin was out of his mind. Now they must have been doubly sure.

From pounding on the jeep with his fist, Carlin graduated to striking me on the leg with all the force he could muster; at the same time literally crying expletives as loudly as he could.

The young fisherman on the jeep started to come to my aid, but I moved my legs out of Carlin's reach and held the fisher-man back.

Carlin continued to rave like a maniac, while everyone stared at him in shocked amazement. Finally he quieted down to where he was only whimpering. Then, abruptly, he released his hold on the back of the jeep and struck out swimming for the fishing ship some seventy-five feet away.

Crewmen on the ship started yelling at him to go back. They didn't think he could make it. He ignored them. When they saw he was going to make it they threw him a line to grab. As soon as he had hold of it, several of them began hauling him up toward the deck.

It was a strange sight—him dangling naked on the end of a rope, like some species of shaggy-headed, four-limbed white fish. When he was finally on deck, he turned back toward the jeep, began shaking his fist at me and yelling in an insane voice:

"You bloody bastard! You male whore! You pimple on a whore's ass!" He repeated each of these expletives three or four times.

The fishermen who had pulled Carlin aboard stood several yards away from him, astonished and probably frightened at his behavior. For one thing, they didn't know what had set him off, and none of them spoke enough English to find out.

Finally they all disappeared into the interior of the ship, leaving Carlin alone on deck; still naked and still screaming curses at me.

The young fisherman who was still aboard the jeep kept asking me, "What's wrong with him? What's wrong with him?"

I told the boy Carlin was drunk, and had gone crazy with cold and rage. Fearing for my safety, the fisherman pleaded with me to leave Half-Safe and go with him to his ship. He did not think I should continue on with Carlin. I was tempted, but I knew Carlin would be his usual pleasant self when the effects of the O'sake wore off.

I assured the fisherman I would be all right. He got into his small boat and rowed back to the ship—going to the side away from the jeep because Carlin was still on deck, as loud and as vile as when he first started.

It looked like he was never going to run down. I climbed inside the jeep and closed the hatch cover. I was half wet, my clothes were getting stiff from the cold, and I had had enough of the whole affair. Then Carlin started off on a new tact. He began calling me by name as if he wanted to tell me something.

There was the possibility he did, so I opened the cover and stood up in the hatch. As soon as my head appeared in the hatchway, Carlin began repeating his choice insults with more vehemence than ever.

Now completely disgusted, I yelled back that he was insane, and waved my hand at him as a signal that I wasn't going to pay any more attention to him. I closed the cover and sat back in the jeep. I could hear his voice for several more minutes; sometimes cursing and sometimes yelling my name. Finally the shouting stopped.

A little later I looked out the window. He had gone inside the ship. He had stood on the bitterly cold, wind-swept deck, naked, and after having worked in the frigid water for over half an hour, and screamed for around twenty minutes. It was the craziest display of stupid, drunken fury I had ever seen.

For the next two and a half hours I sat in the cabin of Half-Safe, listening to the water slap the bottom of the jeep, and the knife-sharp wind whistle and flutter around the air vents and hatch. My wet clothes clung to me. I drank the rest of the O'sake.

I caught myself daydreaming of schemes to get rid of Carlin. It would be so simple, I kept telling myself. I also considered boarding the fishing vessel and leaving Carlin on his own. But I couldn't make myself abandon the jeep and the trip. I had started it and I intended to finish it despite Carlin.

Then I heard my name called again, and looked out to see Carlin, wrapped in a blanket, standing near the railing of the ship. When he caught sight of me he raised his fist into the air and mouthed a new series of his favorite obscenities.

A moment later he dropped the blanket and climbed up on the railing of the ship to jump overboard. Several of the crew members had followed him out on deck and now they tried to restrain him. Two of them grabbed his arms and pulled him away from the railing. Carlin shook them off and again climbed up on the railing. Once again the crewmen grabbed him.

Carlin began to screamed at me: "Tell the bastards to let me go! Tell the bastards to let me go!"

There was, I thought, a good chance he would never come up if they let him jump overboard, but I yelled up to the men: "Let him go!"

I had to repeat this several times and reassure the fishermen over and over that is was all right. Finally they released Carlin's arms and stood back away from him. He climbed awkwardly to the top of the railing, leaned out over the ocean, and dived in. Seconds later he came up blowing like a whale, and struck out strongly for the jeep.

He swam to the back of Half-Safe, climbed aboard and like a half-dead, bearded wolf, crawled on his hands and knees across the top of the cabin and lowered himself into the hatchway, muttering and glaring at me with wild, bloodshot eyes as he went by. Once in the jeep he took up a section of the floorboard and after several minutes of straining, managed to turn the screw about half a revolution with a large hand wrench. Then he started the engine and slipped the propeller into gear.

At first the shaft refused to turn—as it had the night before under the same circumstances. He tried it again and again.

Finally it broke loose. Then very cautiously he revved up the engine and we began to move. Following standard procedure when we took off from a stationary position, I hopped to the rear of the jeep to make sure the fuel tank was clear of the prop, and the tank itself was somewhere behind us instead of in front. The screw seemed to be working normally.

Carlin continued to increase engine revolutions until we were traveling at our usual speed.

It looked like we were going to make it. I waved at the crewmen on the deck of the fishing boat. They waved back. Then I lowered myself into the jeep.

Still naked and shaking as if he were about to fly apart, Carlin motioned for me to take the tiller as soon as I dropped into the seat beside him. He said nothing at all; just glared. He raised up. I slid under him into the seat. Then he dried himself off, put his clothes on and went to bed. About four hours later he stirred, sat up on edge of the bunk, urinated into the can kept for that purpose, and then went back to sleep.

He slept for four more hours and then got up. This was the longest either of us had slept since leaving Japan. It was also the longest watch either of us had pulled. I was about ready to collapse from fatigue.

The first thing Carlin did upon awaking was dump the can he had filled. When he sat back after throwing the urine overboard he said sarcastically:

"The least you can do is throw out your own piss!"

"It wasn't mine!" I said.

Carlin obviously wasn't feeling too well and didn't follow up this pleasant opening for several minutes. Then he asked brusquely: "What course are you on?"

"The same one I've been on for the last eight hours," I said.

This was the signal for a new explosion of obscenity. While still cursing, he shoved the tiller several degrees to one side and shouted: "Hold it there!"

For the next fifteen or so minutes he plotted a new course, then once again grabbed the tiller, setting it himself.

Taking Preventive Measures

Carlin spent the next quarter of an hour eating. When he was done he told me to stop the jeep and follow him outside. I cut the engine and climbed through the hatchway behind him. He began digging in one of the emergency baskets.

"Get the boat hook!" he ordered.

By that time I understood what he was going to do. He had obviously spent some of the last eight hours in the bunk thinking instead of sleeping. A short while later we had the boat hook lashed to the bow of the jeep so its blunt end extended out from the prow about three feet and also about three feet down into the water.

The idea was that the spear-like pole would snare any net we hit and prevent Half-Safe from passing over it. It also meant we had nothing but our hands and feet to keep the fuel tank off of us. But this had become a minor problem since we began encountering the nets.

It was then close to eight o'clock in the evening. About half way through my second turn at the tiller after that, we hit another net. But the make-shift net-guard worked! One instant the hook and bow were clear. The next instant, just as if someone had snapped on a movie camera, the upper section of a net materialized out of the dark water, impaled on that lovely boat hook!

For a split second I was hypnotized by the sight of the net. Then I hit the ignition switch and began scrambling for the hatchway. The sudden silence had awakened Carlin as effectively as would an explosion, and I yelled at him as I was going through the hatch: "We caught a net!"

He followed me out. The boat hook had performed exactly as Carlin planned, spearing the net below the top-rope and raising it up out of the water. We still had the problem of getting across the net without the propeller snagging it—or so we thought. But the wind had taken this problem out of our hands. As soon as we caught the net and the jeep lost power, the wind had begun swinging the rear of the jeep around in the direction in which we had been moving.

By the time we got out on the prow to inspect the net, Half-Safe was beginning to float over it sideways. There was nothing we could do but hold our breath and hope the net would not snag on the wheels or anything else. The few seconds it took us to pass over the net were a lifetime, but we made it.

All there was left for us to do was to disengage the net from the boat hook and wait for the gas tank to follow us over. We looked around. Being lighter since we had removed gas from it and therefore riding higher in the water, the tank had responded to the force of the wind more rapidly than the jeep and crossed the net before we did.

When it was obvious there was no more danger from the net, I restarted the jeep, and swinging in a wide circle to avoid the tank, got us back on course. I was glad Carlin's ingenuity had paid off and couldn't help but congratulate him. He accepted my compliments with a satisfied grin.

Asleep at the Wheel

The rest of the night and all the next day went smoothly. Calling on a tremendous reservoir of strength, Carlin had apparently passed off the effects of his bout with the O'sake bottle and the cold waters of the North Pacific.

For my own part, I still felt tired from the nearly nine hour stint at the tiller. Because of this, I almost steered us into a new kind of disaster.

It was about three in the morning. I had been having trouble staying awake. I tried all sorts of tricks, including singing, counting, thinking about the future and even slapping my face. But about fifteen minutes before it was time to wake Carlin, I felt as if my head had dropped slightly, and I shook it to clear my vision. When I did this I caught sight of something yellow through the side window. There, leaping and diving like a dolphin at play, was the fuel tank—only a few yards away from us!

I practically fainted from the shock. My hand was frozen to the tiller and the thumping of my heart seemed to drown out the roar of the engine. I knew immediately I had fallen asleep and had made at least one full circle and part of another, crossing over the tow line on the way. The fact that we had not fouled the prop on the tow line or collided with the tank itself was sheer, fantastic luck.

Now I didn't know where the line was! From our position in relation to the tank we were probably in the process of passing over it again at that instant. I waited an eternity for the familiar thud from the bottom of the jeep...but it didn't come, and there was the tank riding behind us where it was supposed to be.

My mind wilted with relief. I was suddenly so light-headed I thought I was going to have to hold onto the seat to keep from floating out of it.

As my strength returned, I began to slowly and ever so cautiously put us back on course. For the rest of my watch I had no trouble staying awake.

The Creeping Wall

A few days after the second net collision, we ran into a period of wonderful weather. The bright sun bore down on us from a glittering blue sky and warmed up the jeep. For the first time in many days we were able to leave the hatch cover open. Our clothing and bed gear lost enough of their water so that they were just damp instead of soggy.

One especially warm afternoon, I sneezed. This was the first and last "cold symptom" I was to have during the entire trip.

That night about an hour after I had taken over from Varlin—and about two hours before dawn—we went back to soggy bed clothes again in a matter of seconds.

By this time we were far enough north that on clear, although moonless, nights, the sky never really got dark. There was sufficient contrast between the color of the sea and the sky to provide a sharply defined horizon.

Because of our constant movement in such close proximity to the surface of the sea, however, it was difficult to judge how far it might be to the horizon.

As far as I could tell, that night it seemed to be about half a mile away. I had been glancing up at the horizon for some time and had noted that it appeared to be getting lighter. Then as I watched, the distance to the horizon seemed to be decreasing, slowly at first and then more rapidly.

Finally I was able to distinguish what appeared to be a black wall on the surface of the sea. By that time it was only a few hundred feet in front of us. I leaned forward in the seat, straining to see more clearly. The wall now seemed to be rushing at us at a tremendous speed.

My mouth opened but before I could yell a warning, the black wall was upon us. There was a resounding crash. The jeep bucked and shuddered, and I could feel us being slammed backward and down. A solid sheet of water cascaded through the open hatchway onto the sleeping Carlin. He came out of the bunk sputtering and shaking the blankets. Then he stood up in the hatch and looked around outside for a few minutes.

Half-Safe continued to weave and buck unnaturally for a few seconds, then it settled down.

There was apparently nothing to be seen so Carlin closed the hatch and climbed back into the bunk. Whatever it was, we had met it head-on and suffered no more than a drenching.

During one of his stints in the bunk the following night, Carlin let me know he was awake in a particularly startling way. The sea was fairly rough at the time, and it was hard to keep Half-Safe from yawing like a drunken hippopotamus. I had become numb from trying to keep the compass needle on course but it persisted in veering constantly from three to ten degrees off course to the port side, then on again only to go off to the starboard.

As far as I knew, Carlin was asleep, and I was alone with the steady roar of the engine and the peculiar wallowing noise the jeep made as it sloshed its way through one wave after another. Then, with his mouth only an inch away, Carlin shouted into my ear:

"Get this god-damned thing on course ! "

I jerked to one side as if I had been touched with a hot poker.

He leaned over from the bunk and grabbed the tiller over my hand. "We'll never get there with you running all over the ocean!" he added scathingly. For several seconds he steered the Half-Safe from that position, finally managing to control the yawing a bit better than what I had been doing.

Later, after he took over, I went to sleep. When I awoke and climbed out of the bunk two hours later, he stuck his face up in mine and said in injured triumph:

"That's the way you're supposed to do it!"

He was showing me his eyes. They were puffed up as if he had been struck by some kind of poison, and were so red they appeared to be bleeding. I took his word for it without getting excited. That was the first time his eyes had been in such bad shape, which meant it was also the first time he had tried to do the impossible.

The Happiest Day

Finally, the day I had been waiting for arrived. This was the day we were to make the last transfer of gas from the tank to the jeep, then jettison the tank. It had been my albatross for so long I dreamed about it while sleeping, and was never without the gnawing fear it had either broken loose and left us without sufficient fuel to make land, or that it would somehow contrive to ram us and fatally rupture the jeep.

Since the last gas transfer, it had been riding high in the water and was easier to handle once you got hold of it. But is was also a lot faster and just as dangerous as it had ever been, if not more so.

This time the transfer went fairly smoothly. The hoses were jerked off of the tank nipples a couple of times and the tank wouldn't stay away from the jeep, but there were no waves breaking over the deck and it was not raining. We also had the usual problem of pinched-off hoses but since there was considerably less fuel to transfer, we were able to accomplish the job in a reasonable period of time.

By the time we began removing the holding line and hoses from the tank, I could feel the excitement mounting. I wanted to be finished with the tank in the worst way and could hardly control an urge to pierce it with one vicious thrust of the boat hook. I wanted to see it fill with water and sink to the bottom so there would be no doubt that it was gone.

But no! We were not to be done with it yet! Carlin told me to work it back to the rear of the jeep and hold it there while he checked our position and got out paint and brush. He was going to paint our location on the thing and set it adrift!

My spirits fell like they had been blown out of the air with a cannon. I thought the idea was a waste of time, and might also pose a hazard in case some smaller vessel ran into the tank. I mentioned this but it didn't make much of an impression on Carlin.

Carlin was still stripped from the waist down following the gas transfer, and he now sat down on the rear-end ledge with his legs dangling in the water.

Working carefully because the tank was still dangerous even though empty, I eased the nose of the tank up between his knees. Then I attempted to steady it by holding onto a center eyelet with the boat hook. Carlin braced his legs against the nose of the tank, and also sought to steady it with his free hand. He made some progress with the paint brush each time we were riding up a swell. But when we broke over the top, followed a second later by the tank, a ragged see-saw movement was set up between the Half-Safe and the tank.

At Carlin's instructions, I let go of the boat hook and started taking 16mm movie shots of the scene. While the camera was running, Carlin pretended to going through the motions of painting. It looked like we were going to make it without mishap. But I was over-optimistic.

Carlin became impatient with the way I was rewinding the driving mechanism of the camera and began spitting out some of his favorite adjectives.

I took all his noise and fury to mean I was turning the handle the wrong way, so I reversed directions and unscrewed the handle ! This really got him.

"Give it to me! Give it to me!" he screeched, letting go of the fuel tank and reaching for the camera. As soon as he released the tank it recoiled back on a wave and then shot forward and down when the wave broke...crashing into his right leg. He yelled, grabbed his injured leg, and for the next several minutes sat there rocking and moaning.

When the pain finally subsided, he again exercised some of his choice vocabulary. I had got the handle back on by this time, rewound the camera and was kneeling on the cabin watching him without the least bit of compassion.

My thoughts were: "You asked for it, you son-of-a-bitch, and you got it!"

There were only two figures left to paint. Carlin finally got them on. The tow line was detached from the nose ring of the tank. Then with considerable feeling, Carlin shoved the tank away from us for the last time.

"Be gone you bloody beast!" he said. Then he took the movie camera and got several seconds of the tank drifting away from us, carried along by the wind much faster than it had ever moved before.

But we had removed the tow rope and harness by which the tank had been attached to the jeep, stowed them in one of the wicker baskets on top, and were underway before the tank was out of sight.

Looking back through the rear window, we caught glimpses of the yellow monster for another ten minutes or so when it and the jeep crested a wave at the same time. Finally, it was gone for good.

I knew the tank was gone, but it had been with us for so long and I was so used to it lurking behind and around us like a wild creature just waiting for us to lower our guard that I continued to feel like it was tied to our tail. All the rest of the day I could sense the tank behind us.

In the evening when we stopped to put oil in the engine, I kept wanting to scramble top-side and grab the boat hook. That night I dreamed about the tank. Several days were to pass before I could get the tank out of my automatic reflexes. I was never to rid myself of the nagging feeling that it was still there.

All I had to do was close my eyes and there it would be, bouncing and lunging behind us or circling off to one side, stalking us like a great yellow shark.

Despite my day-and-nightmares, however, the tank was actually gone. This meant we were not only done with protecting ourselves from the tank, but there would be no more gassing up at sea. As the days passed, we began to realize that another nightmare had also become conspicuous by its absence. This was our nightly encounter with the fishing nets. We had finally passed out of the fishing area, and had seen the last of them.

A New Crisis

Things went well for the next few days. Then mid-morning one day Carlin noticed the generator wasn't charging. There was no way of telling how long it had been on the blink or how much charge there was left in the jeep's two batteries.

This was very important because if the batteries were dead, we would never be able to start the jeep's engine again once it stopped.

The situation was serious from two aspects. If the batteries were dead we would not be able to restart the engine even if the generator could be fixed. On the other hand, if the generator could not be repaired, then the batteries would run down in a short time. We would be stranded in either event.

By this time I was do deadened by the routine and rigors of the trip that I could have faced Ahab's Moby Dick without batting an eye. I cannot speak for Carlin's thoughts at the time, but after deliberating for only a few minutes he took the course of the man of action, of the man who had faith in himself and would not give up without giving it everything he had. He looked at me, a kind of wry smile on his face, and said: "Well! Here goes!"

In a swift movement, he turned the ignition switch, killing the engine—an action that was more or less the equivalent of pushing the plunger on a bomb that had two fuses, one of that was set on time and the other one to go off immediately.

If the batteries were already dead or too weak to restart the engine, then for all practical purposes the plunger would hit the instant fuse. If there was still some life in them, then there was a chance the generator could be repaired and we would still be mobile.

There was no way of telling if there was enough charge left in the batteries to start the engine without actually pressing the starter to see if it would kick over. Carlin didn't dare make the test before trying to fix the generator because there might have been just enough juice left for that one start.

He got his tool box out, removed the engine cowling and began working. There was not enough room for me to help him, even if I had known anything about generators—which I did not—so I propped myself up in the bunk and covered my legs with the blankets. Without the engine running, it got cold in the jeep in just a few minutes.

I could have gone to sleep immediately if I had relaxed, but I was sure that wouldn't set right with Carlin.

I sat there and watched him for the next six hours—constantly reminded by the ominous sounds of the sea and wind how lucky I was that the tank was no longer with us.

Because of the position of the generator, more or less under the engine, it was necessary to take it all the way out before it could be worked on. To get it out, Carlin had to virtually hang upside-down. The generator had not been taken off for several years, so the nuts holding it to the engine and the jeep's hull were stuck.

It took a long time to break them loose. Once the generator was out, it required only half an hour or so to clean it, make some adjustments and put it back together again. Re-attaching it to the engine was a lot easier than taking it off had been. Finally when it was in and all the wires had been connected to the terminals, Carlin sat back in the tiller's seat and rested for several minutes.

Then he got ready to touch the starter button. I sat up on the edge of the bunk and leaned over to watch. Now came the pay-off! The engine started or it didn't. If it didn't start we were done. If it did, we still had a chance even if the generator didn't work.

Carlin took a deep breath, let it out, and jabbed the starter button. The engine caught instantly, its deep-throated roar filling the cabin.

By this time I could feel, and I felt like someone had pointed a shot-gun at my stomach, pulled the trigger and had a misfire. Carlin was jubilant, his face wreathed in a wide grin. Then he glanced over at the generator dial, and his grin turned to panic. The needle was lifeless.

The generator wasn't working! Like someone who had suddenly lost his senses, Carlin began flicking his hands across the jeep's control panel, twirling dials and throwing switches so fast I couldn't follow him. Almost as if by magic, the generator needle suddenly came to life and shot over to the charge side of the gauge.

Carlin had switched the gauge off before he dismantled the generator, and had forgotten to turn it back on.

When we got underway there was a faint glow of goodwill in the tight little cabin. It was a relief to me to have some reason for feeling friendly toward Carlin. It had not been his purpose, of course, but he surely had saved my life—at least for the time being.

But this new atmosphere didn't lead to more than a dozen words of conversation. It was much too tiring to make one's self understood over the roar of the engine; and the cold war between us hadn't really thawed that much.

Now we were less than ten days away from our first landfall: the island of Shemya near the tip of the long Aleutian chain. Because we would be relatively close to land for the rest of the journey after Shemya, Carlin decided to get some movie shots of Half-Safe while we were still in the open ocean.

Up to that point it had been too cold, too rough, or we had just escaped some near disaster and he hadn't felt like stopping to take pictures.

The Playful Walruses

Once again Carlin inflated the one-man life raft, stripped from the waist down, and took to the sea on his own—his camera inside a plastic bag in case he got swamped before he got in a position to use it.

As soon as he had drifted some distance away, I was to make passes by him with the jeep so he could get some action shots of the Half-Safe at sea.

The sea was rough but not too dangerous when he made the decision to do the filming. Without some water action the shots would have had no special interest anyway. By the time he cast off in the tiny rubber raft, however, the waves were five to ten feet high and getting higher all the time.

I made several passes at Carlin. He kept waving for me to come in closer. I went by so close he apparently thought I was going to swamp him. When I turned and started in for another pass he was shaking his fist and cursing. By this time it was so rough I could see him only for a few seconds each time I passed. He recognized the danger, and waved for me to pick him up.

I slowed down and started toward him, peering out the side window to avoid running him down. Suddenly he began yelling and pointing. I took the prop out of gear and with engine idling, clambered top-side. Gamboling about the jeep were two of the largest, hoariest bull walruses I'd ever seen.

They were diving under the jeep, going from one side to the other, circling around a few times, and then repeating the same routine.

It was fun until one of them sighted Carlin in his cushion-sized raft about fifteen yards away and charged in his direction. I thought the jig was up and so did Carlin, but the walrus swerved at the last second and went around him. Carlin knew that only a slight brushing would toss him into the heaving sea.

He began paddling with his hands as fast as he could. He made it to the jeep just a few feet ahead of the playful walrus. The walruses stayed with us until we got underway. They were still playing about the same area when we dropped behind the first row of waves.

Over the Side

A few days later we began to see occasional pieces of driftwood, and once had to execute a quick change of course to avoid colliding with a log—sure signs we were approaching land.

By the time we were two days out from Attu, the first island in the Aleutian chain, the amount of debris in the water had increased considerably, and began to cause us trouble.

The jeep's engine was cooled by a heat exchanger which utilized water sucked out of the sea through an intake on the jeep's bottom. One day Carlin noticed the engine was over-heating.

The first thing he checked was the cooling system. As soon as he discovered there was very little water coming out of the run-off hose, he knew what had happened. Debris had been sucked up against the screen covering the water intake, blocking it off.

 Carlin stripped, climbed out onto the prow of the jeep and gingerly lowered himself into the water. The sea was calm for a change and the slight breeze was not especially cold. But the water, as Carlin observed, was like liquid ice. He was shivering as if he were on a vibrator belt, and his lips turned blue after less than two minutes in the water.

Earlier he had worked in the cold water for close to an hour. He commented on the difference, saying he didn't think water could be so cold without turning to ice.

As soon as Carlin had pulled away the leaves, small twigs and bits of seaweed covering the intake opening, water began spurting out of the drainage hose and our problem was solved. We were underway again after a stop of less than twenty minutes.

It was just before noon one day when the top of Attu's highest hill appeared on the horizon as a faint blue-black smudge. The rest of the day passed slowly, marked by an almost imperceptible development of the smudge into a lumpy green island that appeared to be as deserted as the seas through which we had just passed.

At dusk we altered our course slightly and began circling the southern end of the island. By the time we had rounded the southern tip and began moving up along the eastern coast, the sun was sinking behind the island's jutting backbone of hills.

A sprinkling of lights appeared one by one, dotting the gloom on the slope above the beach. For a few minutes Carlin considered heading for the beach near the lights, but we had no idea what or who was on the island or what kind of reception we might receive, so we turned the nose of Half-Safe eastward.

This put the island directly behind us, and looking back it gave the impression we had just left there. For the next two hours, the island remained silhouetted on our rear horizon by the setting sun.

The next day around mid-afternoon we sighted land again. We had been seeing birds all that morning and several times had run into sections of water that were so thick with debris we had to go around them. Carlin suggested there must have been a tremendous storm in the area within the last few days to account for all of the trash.

Despite our efforts to avoid the worst of the floating debris, the water intake clogged up again. For the second time Carlin went overboard to clean it out.

Now we were passing several miles to the south of a long, flat island. The surface of the sea began to smooth over and take on an oily look. We passed some giant rocks that protruded up out of the water like great peaked horns. The atmosphere of the area was completely unlike what we had experienced in the Kuriles.

Now the sea and the birds and the rocks looked alien. In the late afternoon we sighted Shemya, which was to be our first real landfall.

As we approached the island from the west, we began encountering large fields of kelp, and circled around them to avoid fouling the prop. No amount of maneuvering, however, could get us around the seaweed and other trash floating beneath the surface of the water.

Before long, the intake was plugged again. When it became obvious we couldn't proceed without clearing the screen, Carlin looked at me and very quietly and politely said:

"How about you going over this time?"

I was not surprised he asked me; just in the way he asked. It would have been more natural for him to have left me no choice. The idea that I might refuse had never entered my head, but I wouldn't have gone without being asked. I took his behavior as a sign the terrible hardships he had endured were finally beginning to catch up with him.

I removed all of my clothing for the first time in a month, tied a rope around my chest and slid off into the water.

Carlin hadn't exaggerated the coldness of the water. By the time I had been in it for about thirty seconds, the feeling was already leaving my arms and legs, and the back of my neck was growing numb. I was glad of the rope in case I lost the use of my hands altogether.

Fortunately it took only a few more seconds of clawing at the wire mesh covering the intake to free it of the trash. I crawled back aboard the jeep, rubbed myself down with a towel and put my clothes. It was more than two hours before I thawed out and the shakes left me.

End of the First Leg

It took us several hours to work our way around the kelp fields blockading the western approach to Shemya, and we ended up going a number of miles out of our way into the Bering Sea.

Carlin had been in touch with the manager of the Northwest Airlines Station on the island, and had been provided with a map showing a good harbor on the north or Bering Sea side, so we were saved from having to skirt the island again after getting around the kelp.

By the time we were approaching the harbor it was around midnight, but it was still as light as day. The closer we got to shore the more desolate and deserted it looked. The timbers of the piers were rotting and had been smashed by high waves and left un-repaired. All the windows of the buildings we could see had been busted, and the doors sagged open on rusted hinges.

There were no signs of life. Piles of discarded vehicles, rotting tires, scrap lumber and driftwood littered the beach. Wild grass covered the open areas. We came up to shore alongside a pier, but the beach was much too rough for the jeep to negotiate under its own power.

We stood there on Half-Safe for several minutes staring at the dead scene before us and wondering what had happened to the Northwest Airlines facility and the small military unit that was supposed to inhabit the island. Then something on the beach moved. A small Arctic fox, its fur ragged and dirty, trotted out from behind a pile of driftwood, sat down on the beach and stared back at us quizzically.

Carlin dived into the cabin, came up with his 16mm Bolex camera and focused it on the fox.

"May as well get some shots of our welcome committee," he said wryly.

The fox was not afraid of us, and seemed to be waiting for a hand out. But when we threw some stale crackers to it, the fox turned and trotted off. I suggested we had insulted it by the meagerness of our offering.

With or without a reception committee, we had arrived in Shemya, were nearly out of fuel, and needed to replenish our food and fresh water supply. We had no choice but to go ashore and see what we could find. Rather than tie up close to the beach and take a chance on the tide upsetting the jeep, we went back out about a hundred yards, dropped anchor and then tied the nose of the jeep to a pier piling.

When this was done we rummaged our shoes out of the back of Half-Safe, tied them around our necks, then managed to get a line some twenty feet up to the top of the pier and clamber up it. As soon as I set foot on the pier I began to weave like I was drunk, and was prevented from falling flat on my face only by grabbing onto a stack of timber along the edge of the pier.

It was the first time I had been off of the jeep in a month and also the first time I had tried to stand up without holding on to something or being braced against some part of the jeep to compensate for its movements in the water.

Carlin didn't seem to be bothered by the abrupt change from the Half-Safe to solid footing.

"Your balancing mechanism is out of whack," he said.

Still sitting where I had fallen, I put my shoes on—also for the first time in a month. A moment later we began walking down the long pier toward what must have once been a bustling port. We walked past the pier buildings and began, one-by-one, checking other buildings overlooking the harbor.

Some twenty minutes later and about a quarter of a mile from where we started walking, we spotted a light. A last, we thought, now we will find out what is going on. But the light turned out to be over a danger sign on some kind of automatic power station that was boarded over and apparently was not in use.

Leaving the light, we came across a dirt road that showed signs of having been used in the recent past. A vehicle of some sort had been in the port area, so we began following the road, going inland away from the harbor.

After walking for about half an hour we came upon a landing field which appeared to be on the highest part of the island. The field was very large and at one time must have been home for many thousands of men.

We separated. Carlin covered one side of the field, and I covered the other. We found no one and no sign that anyone had been there for years.

While we were still about three hundred yards apart, both Carlin and I spotted another light about a mile off. We began walking toward the light on a course that would bring us together at the far end of the landing field. I arrived at a cut-off road first and instead of waiting for Carlin, kept going.

A few hundred yards on, the road suddenly curved in a wide loop around a field of tall grass. I decided to take a shortcut across the field, judging this would reduce the distance to the light by about half. I had not gone more than a dozen yards off the road when I discovered why it detoured. The tall grass hid a swamp.

I backed off and skirted the swamp, arriving on the far side and climbing back up on the road just as Carlin came around a curve. Seeing me climbing up out of the grass onto the road, he assumed I had gone directly across the center of the field.

In a few seconds he floundered up to his knees, backed off and followed the same circuitous route I had taken. When he caught up with me he was mad.

"Why didn't you tell me that was a swamp?" he grated.

"You could see that it was, couldn't you?" I answered. I still wasn't about to do him any favors. He let the subject drop.

A Nine Day Break

About ten minutes later we arrived at the source of the light. It was a large bare bulb over the door of a low barrack-like building setting in a narrow ravine and nearly hidden by shoulder high grass. There was a sign on the door on which two names had been freshly painted, curtains on the windows and other indications that someone lived there.

Carlin knocked on the door. We stood back and waited for two or three minutes. Nothing happened. He knocked again, louder. A light went on inside and a few seconds later the door squeaked open a few inches. A stubble-bearded, gangly-limbed man in a red night-shirt stuck his face up to the crack and blinked at us.

Carlin leaned forward so his face was about ten inches from the door. "You speak Ruushun?" he asked in a thick accent.

The man blinking through the cracked door rubbed his eyes. "Huh?" he grunted.

"You speak Ruushun?" Carlin repeated.

"HUH?" the night-shirted man grunted again, disbelief in his voice.

Carlin knew he had carried the joke far enough, and quickly explained who we were. Tom Winn, the manager of the North-west Orient Airlines station, had spread the news about our expected arrival. Everyone on the island had been waiting for us for more than a week.

Carlin had estimated it would take us about three weeks to reach Shemya from Wakkanai. It had taken four weeks. As soon as Carlin identified us, the man invited us into his quarters, woke up his partner and telephoned Winn.

The two men we had rousted out of bed turned out to be electricians there under contract to the U.S. Army. Both were from Minnesota, in their fifties and grandfathers many times over. They broke out whiskey and toasted our arrival. They told us we had been reported missing and presumed lost during our last week at sea.

In about ten minutes the NWA station manager arrived in a pickup truck and extended to us the hospitality of the island. He said we could have our choice of rooms in the billets sometimes used by plane crews or passengers during layovers on Shemya.

We piled into his truck and he drove us to our quarters. The two electricians followed in their own vehicle—bringing the whiskey bottle with them. It was then about one o'clock in the morning. We talked and drank for another hour then our hosts left.

There were dozens of rooms in the building in which we were lodged, all of them furnished and ready for occupancy. Carlin and I picked one near the bathroom, and both went immediately to the showers. By this time I was fairly steady while sitting down and weaved only slightly when walking.

I was therefore surprised to find that when I got into the metal-lined shower stall I lost my balance completely as soon as I tilted my head off of a horizontal plane. Each time I started to move around I fell against the shower wall. Finally I resorted to holding onto the cold-water spigot with one hand and washing as best as I could with the other one.

When I eventually crawled into bed to go to sleep, there was another surprise in store for me. No sooner had I laid down on the bunk than I began to feel as if I was back at sea. The bed began to pitch and roll just like a ship in a storm. It got so bad after a few minutes I was afraid I was going to get seasick, and sat up in the bunk.

When the feeling passed I laid down again. The same thing began happening all over. By this time I was so sleepy that after raising up, I leaned against the wall and dozed off. I don't know how long I slept in this position, but when I woke up I was stiff and sore.

Still half asleep, I laid down full-length on the bunk and covered up. The rocking and swaying sensation was still with me, but the bed seemed to have passed through the worst of the storm. I went to sleep.

The next morning we had been up for just a few minutes when the station manager came to take us to a late breakfast. The large dining room was set up cafeteria style. We were told more than 200 men ate there, including the small military unit stationed on the island.

With our bushy beards and jeep-raggled clothing, Carlin and I were quite a spectacle. There were still several dozen diners in the room when we arrived because of the staggered shifts the men worked.

Tom Winn, Northwest Airlines Station Manager, Shemya Island; Carlin; De Mente

Some of the men came up to say a few words to us. The others stared curiously.

After we finished breakfast it was arranged for a bull-dozer to grade an approach from the road down to the beach where we had originally stopped Half-Safe—a distance of about seventy five feet. Then the dozer was to pull the jeep out of the water and up the incline to level ground.

The news of this plan passed around quickly. When we reached the deserted side of the island where we had come ashore, several dozen people were there waiting for us. The bull-dozer had also beaten us there and was then in the process of clearing a private road for us down to the water's edge.

I get ready to throw a tow-line to a man on the beach at Shemya Island. Note the boat hook, still rigged to "catch" Japanese fishing nets. This shot gives a good idea of how small the jeep was and how little deck space there was for moving about.

Carlin and I, followed by several people, walked back out on the pier. The two of us climbed down onto the jeep. When I got the anchor in, Carlin started the engine and began approaching the beach. As usual when we were attempting a landing, I stationed myself on the prow with tow rope in hand, ready to jump off the moment we hit shallow water.

In this case the water was deep enough to float the jeep up to within a few feet of dry land, and I was able to jump ashore without getting wet.

On the first attempt to get close to the water, the caterpillar bogged down, and had to be moved up to more solid ground. Then the tow-rope had to be lengthened in order for it to reach Half-Safe's nose. I passed the bow line to the bull-dozer team.

They quickly made it fast to the dozer, which began moving almost immediately, pulling the Half-Safe up out of the water and on up the beach to level ground.

Carlin and I wait on Half-Safe as the driver of the caterpillar gets into position to pull the jeep out of the water.

In fact, the dozer kept towing us longer than what Carlin wanted it to, and he finally rammed his head out of the hatchway and yelled for the driver to stop. Then we headed back for the NWA facilities on the southwestern tip of the island, parking the jeep on the landing strip near the hangers.

That afternoon Bill Pollack, NWA's public relations director from Minneapolis, showed up to interview us. Carlin drove the jeep up next to a Northwest plane that had landed a short while before. We posed on and about the jeep for several minutes of picture-taking and general questioning.

One of the things Carlin said during the interview was that I had thrown one of his expensive cameras overboard. This was a remark that demanded some explanation. When Carlin refused to follow it up, everyone looked at me.

"That's Carlin's idea of humor," I said, and let it go at that. It was obvious to everyone that something out of the ordinary had happened to the camera, but they took the hint that was implied in my words and manner and went on to other subjects.

Carlin and I greet a stewardess exiting a NWA plane that had just landed on Shemya. NWA's PR director , Bill Pollack, came in on the plane to interview us.

For the next five days we ate, slept and talked. I hit it off with NWA's Ground Control Approach chief John Rohrbough, and Carlin's time was taken up by the station manager, so we saw each other only briefly. I attended a couple of parties given by Rohrbough and his circle of friends, and apparently Carlin was as well taken care of.

One night some time after I had gone to bed, he came in drunk and as was his habit in that state, went to bed on the floor instead of his bunk. His mumbling and banging around woke me up and kept me awake.

After he had been Iying on the floor for fifteen or twenty minutes he said very clearly:

"This is getting serious!" At the same time he raised up, grabbed the comer of my blanket at the foot and began pulling it off of me and covering himself with it. When I felt the blanket starting to slide, I jerked it back out of his hand.

He then reached over, pulled a blanket off his own bunk, and covered up with it.

The next day I happened to return to our room in mid-afternoon. Carlin was there writing what I thought was a letter. It turned out to be a statement to the effect that I agreed to turn over to Carlin my share of any money we might earn as a result of exploiting the trip until the sum reached $400—the value of the camera that had been lost.

I was taken back for a few seconds. It had never occurred to me that I would receive any money for my part in the trip, and the more I thought about it, the more repelling the idea became. I had already agreed with Carlin before leaving Tokyo that I would not write about the trip until at least two years after it was completed.

Signing the statement meant nothing to me, and if I refused I was quite certain Carlin would sue me at the first opportunity. I signed, refused the copy he offered me, and forgot all about it.

About this time, a ham operator on the island got hold of an operator in Phoenix, Arizona where my parents lived. The operator there telephoned my family and completed a connection that allowed me to speak with them for several minutes.

We had been on Shemya for six days when Carlin decided it was time we began preparing to move on. We cleaned Half-Safe, the radio was repaired, and Carlin took the concave filter screen off the water intake on the bottom of the jeep and replaced it with a convex filter.

He figured—correctly as it turned out—that the movement of the jeep through the water would prevent debris from clinging to the convex screen, thereby solving a problem that seemed to be endemic in Aleutian waters.

Carlin had learned from some source before our arrival on Shemya that large gasoline dumps had been left there by the Army and Air Force at the end of the Pacific war. He had reason to believe that many of the drums were still full of perfectly good gas.

The two electricians whom we had met the night of our arrival knew the location of one of the dumps, and agreed to take us there in their station-wagon. The dump was a large one. There were hundreds of drums covering the football-size field about three miles from the air station.

Some of the drums were stacked up yards high. Others were lying on their sides or standing upright...however they happened to fall when dumped from trucks more than ten years before.

We found gas immediately. Every fifth or sixth drum we kicked had some in it. Many were full, and still had the original seals on the caps. But we needed unleaded gas because the jeep's engine ran for day after day at the same speed and temperature. That type of gas was more scarce but within twenty minutes we had located two full barrels.

These were quickly rolled into the station-wagon and hauled down to the pier where we had tied up the first night.

The following morning Carlin was gone when I woke up. I learned later in the day that he, TomWinn, the station manager, and one of the electricians had refloated Half-Safe and were off on a one-day exploration trip of nearby Alaid Island.

When they returned that evening—leaving the jeep in the water moored at the pier—it was soon all over the station that they had got sideways in the heavy surf at Alaid and nearly capsized.

Half-Safe was thrown over on its side by a wave when approaching Alaid Island, near Shemya, tossing NWA's station manager Tom Winn overboard. After landing on the island, a fire was started so he could dry his clothes.

Tom Winn, after his losing match with Half-Safe

To Sea Again

Our ninth day on Shemya we siphoned the gas out of the drums into the jeep' s inboard tanks—an easy undertaking because the top of the pier was some twenty feet above the jeep so all we had to do was insert a large diameter hose into the drums and start the gas flowing. Gravity did the rest.

The next morning we made ready to leave. About fifty people accompanied us to the pier. Carlin climbed down onto the jeep first then I followed him. Supplies were lowered to us in a sling made out of a piece of canvas.

After removing our shoes—to protect the fragile skin of the jeep—I began passing the supplies to Carlin who stood in the well of the hatch.

Perched on Half-Safe's "mainmast," I lower a bag of supplies—
let down on a rope from the 18-feet high pier above— to the top
of the jeep.

While Carlin was storing the supplies inside the Half-Safe I began coiling the various lines on deck and making sure everything that rode outside was in the right place and fastened down. In a few minutes Carlin came out of the cabin and began putting some things in our emergency baskets.

I returned the boat hook to its usual resting place, while Carlin finished stowing supplies. While this was going on, our audience was taking pictures and making the meaningless and sometimes silly remarks people always make under such circumstances.

But Carlin had been listening to these same remarks for several years, and no longer had the patience to accept them for what they were. Finally he couldn't stand it any longer. When one of the men yelled down a particularly inane comment, Carlin shouted: "SAY SOMETHING!" with such force and vehemence the crowd of onlookers was shocked into silence.

From then on, no one said anything to us. After a while the silence got embarrassing. Then we were ready. Carlin descended into the cabin, started the engine and then came back out on deck.

At the same time that he unhitched the nose of the jeep from the pier, I began pulling on the anchor rope which had been thrown out from the rear of the jeep. Since the anchor was fast in the floor of the sea, my hauling in on the line had the desired effect of pulling Half-Safe away from the pier.

When we were over the anchor, it let go of the bottom and I began to reel it in. Now we were drifting free. As luck would have it we drifted into the anchor rope and it became twisted around the propeller shaft. Fortunately, I was able to untangle it

I coil the rope we had used to lower supplies to the jeep from the high pier; Carlin waves to our send-off party. Only a few wave back.

just by reaching down into the water from the back of the jeep. In the process I got my arm and shoulder wet and a bit of water in my right ear, but that was better than having to strip and go all the way in.

I gave Carlin the all-clear signal. He slipped the propeller shaft into gear, revved up the engine and we were on our way—the next stop: Adak, some five days traveling away.

As soon as I had secured the anchor, I went forward on the jeep to take care of the bow line by which we had been moored to the pier. Our send-off party had not yet recovered from Carlin's blast at one of its members, and there were no shouts and little gaiety.

About half of the group seemed to be muttering among themselves, ignoring us. They were not used to eccentric Australians who had been over-exposed to the foibles of the average man, and no doubt considered him an ingrate.

Those we had become closest to, however, waved and did their best to make up for the gloomy atmosphere that had enveloped the party. They were spared too much effort because we were out of sight within a few minutes.

From Shemya we struck an easterly course that kept us in the Bering Sea north of the Aleutian chain. It had been mid-day before we got away from Shemya, and the afternoon passed quickly. For the first several hours we could see the blue silhouettes of islands to our right. This helped the time pass.

That evening we shoved to, and Carlin was able to make radio contact with Shemya. Following his natural inclination to shock people, he tapped out some obscenity over the set.

The Art of Navigation

By the following morning, which broke overcast and foggy, we had already sunk back into the semi-coma state produced by the jeep at sea. Shemya and the nine days we spent there seemed like a dream. The next day the fog settled down in earnest, cutting our visibility to less than fifty feet.

Now the dimensions of our little world had shrunk to a few yards. There was no feeling of progress at all. We seemed to be treading water in a fogged-over goldfish bowl. The only consolation was that with no wind, the sea was calm and although it didn't seem like it, we were actually making good time.

The fog continued on the third and fourth days and was still with us when the fifth day dawned—the day Carlin estimated we would arrive in Adak. About ten o'clock in the morning, the blanket of fog shrouding us suddenly became solid, and we could barely see the nose of the jeep.

Fearful that we might flounder on some rocky beach or collide with something in the water, Carlin ordered our speed reduced.

We continued under these circumstances for about four hours, at which time Carlin ordered another reduction in speed. With a regular cruising speed of only two knots per hour, that meant we were moving just enough to keep Half-Safe on course.

Carlin had been standing in the hatchway checking our charts and the progress we had made since leaving Shemya. Finally he ducked into the cabin, put the charts away and said rather nonchalantly:

"Adak should be right over there." He pointed off to our right.

For the next fifteen minutes we crept along, more or less waiting. For what, we were not quite sure. Then, as if it had all been arranged in advance, the fog lifted. One moment it was there and the next moment it was gone.

About five hundred yards to our right, the blue waters of the Bering Sea breaking against rocky cliffs, was Adak.

Except for a few minutes one afternoon, we had traveled blind for five days and accomplished the equivalent of a perfect bull's-eye without being able to see the target. I congratulated Carlin on his navigation.

Shortly after the fog bank lifted, a U.S. Navy patrol plane flew over us. It was the first plane we had seen in the air since leaving Japan.

Adak Island

The harbor of Adak is located deep inside a funnel-shaped bay which extends in a gentle curve back into the island. On each side of the mouth of the bay is a high, peaked promontory. We could see the nearest of these entrance markers from our position when the fog lifted.

Using the peak as a guidepost, we set our course for the harbor. It took about an hour to reach the mouth of the bay, and then another forty-five minutes to travel its length.

This was no Shemya. The harbor was bustling with activity. There were ships everywhere. When we were still several hundred yards out, a group of people gathered at the central dock and waved us to proceed to a small boat landing near where they were standing.

I dropped the anchor when we were about fifty yards out from the dock, and then scrambled forward and scooped up the bow line. Carlin eased the jeep up to the dock. I tossed the line to willing hands and they tied us up.

Carlin shut the engine down, we put our shoes on and started to climb up on the dock. At that time a Navy officer appeared and told us to stay where we were until he got official clearance for us to come ashore. For the next twenty minutes or so we sat on the softly bobbing jeep, waiting for the station's commanding officer to be found.

It turned out that the Navy patrol plane that had flown over us earlier had reported the jeep as an unidentified submarine approaching the harbor with conning tower showing!

Waiting on a pier at Adak Island, a U.S. anti-submarine base, for permission to land.

Carlin had notified the base commander by letter that we would be coming through the area, and when he was finally reached, he immediately invited us ashore and gave instructions that we were to be guests of the station. We were quickly shown to quarters in an officer's billets and give the freedom of the island.

One of the first things we did was contact the representative of Reeves Aleutian Airways, an airline operating along the chain from Anchorage. Bob Reeves, the famous bush-glacier pilot and founder of the airline, had agreed earlier to act as a mail-drop for us and to fly our mail out to Adak first, then as we progressed up the chain, to Cold Bay.

There was mail waiting for both of us. During the next two days we took care of our correspondence, were interviewed by the local closed circuit television station, and feted by the Reeves representative and other personnel on the island.

When Carlin raised the subject of gas, the Navy agreed to sell us some for a token price. But Carlin was sure there would be dumps on the island, just as there was on Shemya, where we could find perfectly good gas going to waste.

Much to the surprise of the people who volunteered to help us, the search was successful, and we soon had all the unleaded gasoline we needed. Because the gas we found was still American property and on a U.S. Navy base—even if no one on the base knew about it—Carlin agreed to pay for the gas we took.

The money he offered was first accepted but very soon returned. Finding the gas and getting it to the dock-side proved to be easy and unexciting, but siphoning it into the jeep's tanks produced fireworks—as usual-between Carlin and myself.

Once again the dock was high above the jeep and there was no special problem involved in making the transfer. But in order to get all of the gas out of each drum, it was necessary to tilt them over on one edge and balance them there.

I was on the dock with a sailor helping me. Because the tap in the drums was on the side, and small, it was difficult to tell where the end of the hose was that we had inserted into them. In swishing one of the hoses around to make sure it was in the deepest part of the barrel, it lost contact with the gas.

Of course, the flow of fuel through the hose stopped. When Carlin, down on Half-Safe, saw the gas slowing to a trickle he yelled up:

"Is that all?"

"No," I replied. "The hose came out of the gas but there are about two gallons left."

"You god-damned incompetent son-of-a-bitch!" he screamed. "What am I going to do with you?"

I knew it would add to his fury, but I said it anyway. "You can leave me on Adak."

"You son-of-a-bitch! You son-of-a-bitch!" he chanted vehemently.

He knew better than I did that one man alone of the jeep would very likely be committing suicide. My indifferent suggestion brought his volatile temper to the boiling point instantly.

But the possibility that I might decide on my own to resign from the often unpleasant enterprise must have occurred to him, because he quieted down much faster than usual.

Later Carlin decided he wanted to check the bottom of the jeep, and after looking around the harbor we located an area where the beach was a gentle slope and there was a hard, gradually ascending bottom.

We drove the jeep out of the water without incident—only the second time this had been accomplished so far without help. The next morning we made ready and boarded the jeep, which lumbered off into the harbor like a tame hippopotamus.

On the way out of the harbor we chugged past ship after ship of bug-eyed sailors who, after seeing the Half-Safe, must have felt a little better about the ships they put to sea on. Forty-five minutes later we were back in the open ocean.

Our next stop, only three days travel this time, was the island of Umnak, well-known along the chain for its large sheep ranch owned and operated by the Harris family.

Through the Boiling Sea

Rather than lying straight east of Adak, Umnak is off to the south a bit. In order to approach it from the Bering Sea side of Adak where we were, it was necessary to pass through the island chain into the North Pacific.

Carlin had plotted our course to take us through the chain by way of a narrow channel just east of Adak. When our newfound friends on Adak heard this, they were aghast. That particular channel was a death-trap that had been notorious for several hundred years. Only ships above a certain tonnage were considered big enough to challenge its awesome rip-tides.

They thought Carlin was crazy when he insisted we were going through it and didn't anticipate any trouble. I must confess to some initial concern, but I kept reminding myself that in addition to other things, Carlin was an expert on what the jeep could and could not do and not many men knew the sea better than he did.

Reassured by this reminder, I began looking forward to seeing and experiencing this infamous ship's graveyard.

We were not disappointed with our first glimpse of the passage. It was about three miles in width, and we approached it almost dead center. I had expected that we would gradually get into rough water and that it should get worse as we neared the main collision point of the two tides. But this was not the case at all.

On a line almost as precise as the white stripe down the center of a highway, the sea changed from a placid blue to a boiling cauldron. When we crossed the line, I held my breath. It was like sailing off a calm lake onto the top of a geyser spout so gigantic one couldn't see where it ended.

I braced myself, expecting the jeep to immediately begin pitching and rolling wildly. But it didn't. There was so little reaction I nearly fell off the jeep in surprise. When the full length of Half-Safe had passed into the frothy, roiling white water, it shuddered slightly and began to buck just enough to make the ride interesting.

There was nothing else. I couldn't believe it. I asked Carlin why there wasn't more reaction to a sea that appeared to have gone mad. He smiled at the question but as far as I can recall, did not answer.

It is my opinion that because of the shallow draft of the jeep we did not sail through the riptides. We sailed across the top of them on the bubbles and foam stirred up by the terrible clashing of the waters deeper down. The tide-rip field ended as abruptly as it had begun, and we were once again on blue water.

Adventures on Umnak

We had good sailing weather from the tide channel to Umnak, and began approaching the island within half an hour of the time Carlin had predicted. The Harris home was located on the southwestern side of a large shallow bay, and we headed in that direction.

From the mouth of the bay to its head was about four miles. The Harris's spotted us a long time before we got near their home. When we pulled up about a hundred and fifty feet out from the beach, the Harris's and several Aleut children were there to greet us.

The beach was too steep for us to attempt a land, so we dropped anchor. Mr. Harris immediately began pushing a small dorrie into the water to come out and ferry us in. This was no easy task since he had only one arm, but he made it, and we were soon ashore and sitting in the Harris' living room.

A few minutes and two or three drinks after our arrival, a U.S. Army vehicle pulled up outside the Harris house. There were two men in the truck, from a construction crew that was building some military facilities on the island. The men invited us to be their guests for as long as we wanted to stay on Umnak.

They had heard about our landings at Shemya and Adak, and had been waiting for us.

Their construction camp was located on top of a promontory overlooking the mouth of the bay. They had spotted us a few minutes after we entered the lagoon-like bay. We had already been invited by the Harris's to stay with them, but after a brief comparison of the two invitations we decided to put up with the construction men.

The Harris home had only two bedrooms, and our presence would have imposed a hardship on them. The two men left, saying they would send a truck for us later that evening.

In addition to the Harris', their daughter, Patti, a hired hand and the construction team, Umnak was also home to a small group of Aleutian natives, or Aleuts. The Aleut village was composed of some twenty houses set haphazardly overlooking the beach at the head of the bay.

The Harris home was on a slight rise about a hundred and fifty yards to the right of the village. All but half a dozen of the men and older boys of the village were gone—off fishing or working at some other occupation on other islands.

After dinner that evening, we heard shouting coming from the beach. Mr. Harris explained that some of the villagers had taken a drag net out a hundred feet or so from the beach, lowered it into the water and were now pulling it in. I went down to watch.

The net was small, but the catch amounted to several baskets of different kinds of fish. They were quickly divided up, expertly cleaned there on the beach and then carried away by the Aleut women. One of the men presented me with three beautiful specimens to take back to Mrs. Harris.

Shortly afterward, the vehicle from the construction camp arrived to pick Carlin and me up. The camp was set up something like a small military installation, with barracks and adjoining mess hall. We were shown to private rooms and told to make ourselves at home.

There was a movie that night in the mess hall, and we went to see it. The next morning after breakfast, the construction chief showed us around the camp. Then we returned to our rooms to write letters.

At noon I went to the mess hall, expecting to see Carlin there, but he didn't show up. I asked one of the men with whom we dad talked several times if he had seen Carlin.

"Yeh ! I saw him a couple of hours ago," the man said. "He got pissed off at something somebody said and jumped into a truck that was going down to the village. What kind of an odd-ball is he anyway?"

I didn't try to answer the man's question. There wasn't much possibility Carlin was planning on leaving so soon, but since I really didn't know what he might have decided to do, I began looking for a ride for myself. An hour or so later a truck dropped me off at the village.

The jeep was still anchored where we had left it. Carlin was nowhere in sight. I went up to the Harris house. Mrs. Harris invited me in. She said Carlin had shown up earlier that morning and gone off with her husband on a tour of the ranch.

Mrs. Harris made coffee, and we sat and talked for several hours. She and her husband had been on various of the Aleutian islands for more than twenty years, and knew almost everyone along the chain. Their means of keeping up with their island neighbors and the outside world was a powerful short-wave radio set built into the wall of their living room.

In addition to daily reporting the weather to the nearest Coast Guard station, they also functioned as a communications center for anything else that happened on the island or pertained to it.

Mrs. Harris had written up the ranch and their lives on Umnak for *Reader's Digest*, and showed me some of the thousands of letters she had received after the article appeared.

The Harrises had built their home on a spot that afforded a beautiful view of the long bay. To take advantage of the view, the side of their living room facing the sea was mostly glass— nearly an inch thick and reinforced to withstand the fierce gales which frequently sped in from the Bering Sea and whipped the island for days at a time.

After we had been talking for a while, Mrs. Harris mentioned Carlin. "I don' t know what you think of him or how you get along," she said, "but I think he is a bit weird. Aren't you afraid of what he might do?" she asked.

The idea had certainly occurred to me but I didn't think it was that serious, and told her so. Then she went on to describe a scene she had witnessed that morning. As was her custom, she had been sitting in front of the window looking out over the bay with a set of powerful field glasses.

"I saw a truck coming down off the hill from the construction camp. Just before it got to the village, it stopped very suddenly and Carlin jumped out, apparently having a row with the driver. The truck continued on, leaving Carlin beside the road. He walked around a bit then went over near a pile of lumber, dropped his trousers and proceeded to relieve himself there in the open. I can still see his white backside shining in the sun!"

We talked on for a while then I went down to the village. One of the younger men was on the beach. After a while he invited me to his home. His house was small and sparingly furnished with old chairs and tables roughly made. He introduced me to his mother. They seemed to me to be a sad people, not pliable or strong enough to cope with the modern world. There was something about the texture of their flesh and the sluggishness in their eyes that reminded me of death and decay. They seemed, however, to be a kind and gentle people.

Shortly after Carlin and Mr. Harris returned from their tour of the island ranch, we had dinner. Afterward, we sat around drinking and talking. Or that is, Carlin and Mrs. Harris talked.

For once Carlin had met his match in the use of invective and obscenity. They were already at it before we left the dinner table. Mr. Harris and I sat back and listened. There was nothing Carlin could say that Mrs. Harris couldn't shred to bits in a few swift words.

There were no words he could use that she couldn't make pale in comparison. And finally, when their voices began to rise, she out-shrilled him in a way that only a woman could.

This went on for more than an hour, and at last Carlin had all he could take. He was practically foaming at the mouth with bile and spleen, but he swallowed it with an effort that must have cost him dearly, and gave up the battle.

I had enjoyed every second of his crucifixion on his own tongue as it were, and had not been so pleased since we jettisoned the fuel tank. About midnight I called it quits, crawled up a ladder into the Harris' attic den and went to sleep on a cot.

Carlin and the Harrises continued drinking until just before dawn, and then Carlin went to sleep on the living room couch. By ten o'clock he was stirring and we made ready to leave.

Mrs. Harris and several of the villagers accompanied us to the beach to see us off. Mr. Harris had been called away by his hired hand. The villager who had invited me into his home rowed us out to Half-Safe and we climbed aboard.

Carlin was suffering from a hangover and ill-humor, and didn't have anything to say. I waved farewell to our send-off party and then signaled Carlin I was all set to haul in the anchor. He punched the started button. The engine kicked over, started, spluttered and then stopped.

This was repeated twice more. Then Carlin removed the cowling from the engine and began checking the carburetor. I stuck my head into the cabin.

"What's wrong?" I asked him.

"Dirty carburetor," he answered shortly. I sat back on the cabin top and relaxed, expecting that he would have the carburetor cleaned and back in working order in twenty minutes or so.

I yelled the news to Mrs. Harris and the rest or our audience. They also took it for granted the delay would be for only a few minutes, and continued standing on the beach watching us.

After about half an hour, Mrs. Harris gave up and went back to the house.

There was a chilly breeze blowing and what sun there was had gradually disappeared behind sullen, grey clouds. Another twenty minutes and the villagers also drifted away. An hour and a half passed.

Mrs. Harris, sitting in her picture window, pointed to her watch in a questioning manner as if to ask, "How much longer?" I shrugged my shoulders.

Carlin was probably among the world's greatest auto mechanics. There was no doubt about his being the slowest. Then Mrs. Harris made a sign asking me if we wanted to come back to the house to eat lunch—it was then around one o'clock. I shook my head no.

About two o'clock, some two and a half hours after we had boarded Half-Safe, Carlin signaled for me to get back on the anchor line. He pushed the starter button. This time the engine caught and began purring like a well fed lion. I started hauling on the anchor rope, pulling us back away from the shore.

When the anchor broke the surface, Carlin geared up, swung the jeep around and we were off. I waved at Mrs. Harris and the few children playing around on the beach.

The bay got wider as it neared the mouth, and instead of heading down the center channel by which we had come in, Carlin began angling off to the right, intending to save a mile or two.

About five hundred yards out we suddenly ran into shallow water and before we could do anything about it, the jeep's wheels—which stuck down about two feet lower than the hull—began colliding with submerged rocks. We bounced from one rock to another until Carlin was able to cut our speed.

I jumped from the cabin down to the doll-sized prow to guide him around the worst of the rocks.

We finally had to back up and do a considerable amount of zig-zagging to reach the channel. Once we found it there was no further difficulty, and again Half-Safe had suffered no apparent damage as a result of the buffeting it had taken from the rocks.

Smooth Sailing & Whales

Late that afternoon, in a calm sea with blue-black islands visible on both sides of us, we spotted a whale pod several hundred yards off to our right. There were twenty or more of the great mammals cruising along leisurely on a course almost parallel to ours.

We watched them for close to an hour, wishing they would come in a little closer and give us a better view, but at the same time relieved that we didn't have to worry about being run down by them.

A number of the larger whales had more than twenty feet of back showing out of water. We knew there was lot more on both ends of this. Our seventeen feet wouldn't have impressed them very much.

Stop-Over at Unalaska

The day after leaving Umnak and the Harris Sheep Ranch, we arrived at Unalaska and pulled into Dutch Harbor located on a small islet inside Unalaska Bay. In addition to various port facilities for larger ships, we soon found a concrete slip-way leading up out of the water onto a blacktopped airstrip.

Driving up out of the sea was no more difficult than pulling a car over to the side of the road and parking it.

Dutch Harbor! That had been a name that meant something during the early Pacific War years. Then, more than a hundred thousand men at one time or another had called the place home for a little while. The bay was full of ships during those years, and the tremendous complex of buildings around the port, on the hills overlooking the harbor, and on the adjoining main island of Unalaska, were filled with busy people.

When we pulled ashore, cut the jeep's engine and climbed out, we were struck by the feeling that always seems to pervade a ghost town. There was a wind-direction flag flapping in the breeze above a terminal building along-side the runway, and we could hear the waves lapping against the shored-up sides of the waterfront airstrip.

We began exploring. Several buildings around the runway were locked up and their windows were intact—an indication they were still used at least occasionally. Peering through the windows into dark interiors, we saw a number of offices that still looked in order. But there was no sign of anyone.

We left the airstrip and began systematically checking other buildings lining regular paved streets around the harbor. There were barracks, office buildings, a theater and even a library three stories high and covering nearly a square block.

Everywhere we looked windows were broken and doors were gone or hung open on single hinges. The interiors of the buildings had been stripped. The only thing left was the wall paper, and rats—many thousands of them, living on paste that had held square miles of paper to the walls of countless buildings.

When we reached the south end of the island within an island, we found a small-boat pier. I saw a ball-peen hammer sticking in the sand a few feet out of the water, and fished it out. It had never been used, and except for the handle looked like new. The salt water had bleached the wooden handle almost white.

The center of the islet was made up of a ridge of low, rounded hills. The main street we had taken out to the harbor area continued on around the island along the beach. We decided to follow it around since the island wasn't more than two miles in circumference.

Coming around behind the low hills opposite the harbor we saw smoke spiraling up from two chimneys on top of the hill. We made our way through tall grass and molding trash dumps toward the two houses.

There was no one in the first house we went to, although someone obviously lived there. Just when we began to approach the second house, a vehicle pulled up and a man got out.

We introduced ourselves to him and learned that he was the representative of an American oil company which still had some facilities on the island. He had returned to his quarters from the main island to pick something up, and offered to take us back with him.

We waited until he ran into the house for a few minutes, then piled into his car and went to another small boat harbor on the back side of the islet. After a few minute boat ride we tied up a pier adjoining the settlement of Unalaska.

The settlement had a mixed population of perhaps two hundred, made up of native Aleut islanders, pioneer Alaskans and a contingent of Army personnel assigned to a permanent weather station on the island.

The buildings and homes were made of wood. Those in the center of the settlement were old. One of them, said to have been the official residence of the last Russian governor of the territory, was being used as a hotel by the woman who owned it.

Following introductions, that is where Carlin and I were lodged as guests for the night.

When we had first landed on Shemya some three weeks earlier, I had noticed something different about the island, about its vegetation and atmosphere. This sense of something peculiar had grown increasingly stronger as we moved up the chain, first to Adak, then Umnak and now Unalaska.

That night after I went to bed I tried to analyze what it might be. In the early morning the islands appeared to be a new lost world that civilization had passed—possibly because they were hidden behind fog banks so much of the time.

Then in the evening, this new untouched atmosphere faded and was soon replaced by an eerie appearance of age and decay. The islands appeared to have lost their vitality and been abandoned. I decided the solution to the puzzle was the position of the sun in the sky at different times of the day. That far north it never got very high in the sky at any time. Its rays always struck the islands at a low angle.

In addition to this light phenomenon, there was a luxuriousness about the vegetation that suggested something wild as long as the vegetation was alive and growing. In contrast, any tree or plant that was dead looked like it had been dead for centuries. Any unpainted wooden surface was bleached a hoary grey in a matter of months.

The next morning we learned that a plane from Anchorage, on its way to the Pribiloff Islands with a group of tourists who wanted to photograph the seals, was scheduled to make a refueling stop at the airstrip where Carlin and I had left the jeep. The oil company representative invited us to go along with him to meet the plane.

In the meantime, Carlin had decided to sail the jeep around to the settlement so the kids could see it, and readily accepted the boat ride back to Dutch Harbor.

We arrived at the airstrip several minutes before the plane was due, but it came in on time carrying mail for Unalaska, some fifteen tourists for the seals on the Pribiloffs, and a press photographer from the *Anchorage Times*. Carlin took some pictures of the tourists, and they got some shots of Half-Safe.

A few minutes after the plane left, we drove the jeep off the slip-way and chugged out into the harbor. It took us about twenty minutes to sail around the south end of Dutch Harbor and approach the landing at Unalaska Settlement.

A speed boat cavorting in the bay facing Unalaska crossed our path several times and got a rise out of Carlin, but we reached the small boat harbor without mishap and were soon tied up to the pier.

During the next several hours, most of the inhabitants of the island went down to see the jeep and photograph it. A number of kids kept permanent watch over it.

More Smooth Sailing

That afternoon we made ready and were soon trundling out of the bay past Dutch Harbor and into the North Pacific. Our next major stop was to be Cold Bay on the Alaska Peninsula, our first contact with continental U.S.A.

Now began one of the most interesting and comfortable periods of the trip. Our course from Unalaska took us winding through a maze of channels separating a number of little islands. There was very little wind, and the sea was as smooth as if it had been rolled. The horizon in every direction was decorated with picturesque blue-grey islands.

Late in the afternoon, while cruising between two long islands in a northerly direction, we spotted a sea-wall and lighthouse on the island to our left. Carlin' s chart showed some kind of settlement there. He decided to go exploring. The lighthouse marked the entrance to a narrow but fairly long cove.

As soon as we were inside the cove, we found ourselves in a strange, isolated world. On the hillside to our right (the side catching the rays of sun) was a number of attractive houses of the type on sees in southern California. Below the houses was a boat landing.

Smoke was wafting up from the chimneys of the houses, but there was no one in sight. We steamed up to the landing and there found an old man working on a boat.

We laid over for about an hour talking to the man and eating. He told us the men living in the cove all had boats with which they earned their living. At that time they were all gone.

There was nothing to be gained from staying in the cove any longer than we already had. The old man had said there was a fairly large settlement at a cannery a few miles further on. We decided to make for that.

We made that landing just at dusk and tied up alongside a good-sized fishing ship which had just finished unloading at the cannery. The bay on which the cannery was located was hardly more than a pocket in the shore. There were a few houses, a store and barracks where the cannery workers lived.

I went ashore and looked over the general trading store which was a few hundred feet from the pier. Carlin went aboard the fishing boat to talk to the crew.

We were only a day's travel from Cold Bay, and Carlin announced that we would lay over at the cannery until midnight to take advantage of the tide. As a matter of fact, we had no choice but to wait for the tide. When it started ebbing, it came out of Cold Bay at a much higher speed than what Half-Safe could move.

Rather than spend the evening talking, I told Carlin I was going to turn in and try to get some sleep. One of the ship's officers loaned me an alarm clock, which I set for eleven-thirty. I was asleep in two minutes.

When the alarm went off I climbed aboard the fishing boat and was invited to help myself to coffee. At almost exactly midnight we upped anchor and headed out across the open channel separating the Aleutian Island chain from the Alaska Peninsula.

It took us the rest of the night and all the following morning to cross the channel and approach the mouth of Cold Bay. The early afternoon found us rounding the long sand-bars that make much of the mouth impassable by anything larger than a rowboat.

Nightfall came and we were still several miles out. A wind sprang up and it got cold.

At Cold Cold Bay

Some time around midnight we reached the port area of Cold Bay but now the wind was blowing with the force of a gale. Rather than take a chance on tying up in the main harbor, Carlin chose to make for a small lagoon-like area behind a long pier, which set up on pilings some thirty feet above sea-level, as protection against high waves.

It took us about half an hour to go around five hundred yards. Then when we got behind the pier we found it was just as unprotected as the open-sea side. Now the wind was blowing so fiercely Carlin was afraid to take the jeep in close to the pier for fear we would be smashed against the pilings.

There were no lights to be seen anywhere and because of the noise of the wind, we knew there was no use trying to attract anyone's attention by calling.

Finally we dropped anchor in the center of the wind-swept lagoon and prepared ourselves to wait out the night. When it became apparent the anchor was going to hold the jeep, we took turns sleeping until dawn. Instead of abating during the night, the wind seemed to have become stronger with the coming of day.

About an hour after dawn, we saw signs of life. A truck came down off a low hill facing the harbor and drove out on the quarter of a mile long pier. The driver of the vehicle must have spotted us as he went by, because a few minutes after he reached a large complex of warehouses at the end of the pier, he and two other men jumped back into the truck and drove at high speed until they were opposite us on the high pier.

They got out of the truck and began waving and shouting. Like everyone along the island chain, they knew who we were and had been expecting us.

With someone there to help us, we would now be able to tie up to the pier without having to get too close to it. I took off my socks and trousers to keep them dry, went out on the prow of the jeep and began readying a throwing line. The wind was howling fiercely, driving ice-cold spray off the cresting waves in stinging sheets. The men on the pier, dressed in heavy coats, hoods and gloves, watched the operation in respectful awe.

When the bow line was ready I scrambled to the rear of the jeep and began hauling in the anchor. The moment it broke free of the bottom, Carlin began easing the jeep toward the pier.

When we were about sixty feet out I dropped the anchor, line and all, a few yards to the rear of the jeep and then raced to the prow, grabbed up the throwing line and braced myself to heave it to the men on the pier as soon as we were within distance.

The first several attempts to approach the pier were unsuccessful . The wind kept blowing us off to one side. All of this time, I was balanced precariously on the prow, half naked, the sub-freezing wind drenching me with spray every few seconds.

When it began to look like we weren't going to be able to get close enough for me to throw the line, the men on the pier signaled for us to give up and try on the other side of the pier.

They did not stop to consider that if we came in from the other side, the wind would probably smash us into the pilings before we could anchor, and after tying up a the pier—if we succeeded in doing that—it would still be the anchor line holding the jeep and that might let go at any time.

If we ever managed to get tied up where we were, at least the strain would be on the line fastened to the pier. After more than half a dozen attempts to get Half-Safe within twenty feet or so of the pier, Carlin finally made it and I let fly with the line.

Fortunately the toss was good and the men soon made us fast. I returned to the cabin of the jeep, dried off and put my clothes back on. Then by pulling on the bow line we hauled the jeep up to where we could get a foot-hold on the pilings and with the aid of a rope let down by the men above us, climbed onto the pier with our shoes hanging around our necks.

As soon as we let go of the bow line, the force of the wind shoved Half-Safe back out until it hit the end of the rope with a loud pop. The line held. The jeep hung there, rearing and plunging in the high waves.

In addition to being a regular stop-over for military planes and Reeves Aleutian Airways, Cold Bay was also an alternate landing field for Northwest Airlines planes bound for Japan. It was also an important stop-over for inter-island shipping, and headquarters for a number of government functions, including Immigration.

It was still early and bitterly cold when we left the jeep. The men who had help moor us to the pier gave us a lift to the joint NWA-Reeves mess hall, where we were first in line for breakfast. Later we picked up our mail at the Reeves terminal, and the rest of the day sat around answering correspondence and drinking coffee.

The following morning the wind had died down and there was a warm sun shining. A Reeves pilot invited me to drive out to a nearby lake with him and fly a small amphibian plane back to the airstrip. He had flown the plane in two days before but fog had forced him to land at the lake about fifteen miles from the bay.

It took about half an hour to drive to the lake. We boarded the plane immediately. He started the engine, let it warm up for about five minutes, then we took off. We were back at the airstrip in less than three minutes.

At noon a Reeves passenger-cargo plane came in from Anchorage. Carlin offered one of the stewardesses a ride on Half-Safe. The three of us climbed down on the jeep from the pier. Then with Carlin and the girl inside the cabin, we steamed out from behind the pier into the open bay. We went about a mile out, then began moving in a large circle toward a crescent-shaped sandy beach south of the pier.

When we were still about a quarter of a mile out, I yelled to Carlin that we were coming into shallow water fast.

Less than thirty seconds after I shouted the warning, we hit bottom, Carlin switched to wheel-drive and let the clutch out, but the bottom was soft sand. A moment later we were hopelessly mired up to the axles.

The predicament wasn't particularly dangerous but there was no way we could get the jeep out under its own power or get another vehicle out there to pull us in. We were stuck in the sand until the tide came in some six hours later.

We threw out the anchor and got ready to abandon jeep—at least temporarily. Carlin and I took our trousers off and slid into the water from the rear of the jeep. The stewardess had slacks on and decided to keep them on when she followed us a moment later.

The water was just a few inches above the knees when we stepped off of Hal-fSafe, but on the way in we hit small depressions where it was deeper. The girl got wet well past her hip pockets. Once ashore there was nothing to do but wait for the tide.

We returned to the air crews' quarters and spent the rest of the afternoon talking. Earlier that morning our passports had been checked—but not stamped—by the local Immigration representative. That evening some of the men volunteered to drive us back to the beach about half a mile away.

Again Carlin and I stripped down to wade back out to Half-Safe. By the time we reached the jeep, the water was up to our chests. We climbed aboard, dried off and redressed. Then I pulled anchor. As soon as I gave Carlin the all-clear signal we headed for the beach at full speed. Carlin had decided to take the Half-Safe ashore for the night.

Close in, the sand had been beaten down and when we hit bottom this time—only a few yards from shore—the wheels caught and we came up out of the water like a charging rhino.

We did not hit the beach squarely, however, and came out at an angle. That in itself was no problem but we came out at near the tide-water limit and immediately landed in soft sand.

Carlin knew the jeep would bog down if he stopped, so he kept going, running parallel to the beach looking for hard ground. When he judged it was safe enough he began to slow down.

As soon as he did the wheels started sinking. In the meantime I had jumped off the jeep and was running alongside, accompanied by one of the men who had driven us to the beach. We began yelling for Carlin to keep going. He tried but it was too late.

He was about six feet from firm ground when Half-Safe gave up and sank back on its haunches.

The tide wasn't all the way in yet and we didn't know exactly how far it would come, so we started digging the jeep out. First we dug trenches in front of the wheels, and tossed pieces of waste lumber into them. But all the wheels would do was spin. We changed one piece of driftwood for another and added some other pieces of trash. This combination also failed.

By this time it was dark and difficult to see what we were doing. The men who were helping us finally hitched their truck to the jeep, we worked new planks under the rear wheels, and tried it again.

The third time, Carlin and the truck driver got their gears synchronized and the Half-Safe crawled up out of its self-made grave. The road leading from the beach up to the Cold Bay settlement was too steep for the jeep to negotiate, so we closed the hatch and left it there.

About 2 a.m. that night, Carlin and I got up and went down to check on it.

A hospital ship that cruised among the islands had docked in Cold Bay the day after our arrival. We were invited to have lunch with one of the officers the day following the grounding of Half-Safe.

The ship was having difficulty getting enough operating funds from the Alaskan Government and was understaffed. To me, it appeared virtually abandoned.

Shooting Shellikof Straits

Late that afternoon we boarded Half-Safe and began the next leg of our journey. To prevent us from bogging down on the beach again, Carlin gunned the jeep across the fifteen yard ribbon of soft sand and we hit the water like a gooney bird running amuck.

It was dark before we got out of sight of the harbor facilities and dawn the next morning found us just approaching the mouth of the bay. We didn't have to guess about the time we left the bay and entered open water. The wind was blowing with close to gale force and the sea was heaving as if it were sick.

Strangely enough, the wind was not disturbing Cold Bay this time. Instead it was pouring down Shellikof Straits as if it were shooting through a wind tunnel.

By noon, or an hour or so after we sighted the western tip of Kodiak Island, the jeep was bucking and see-sawing more than it had any other time since we left Japan. Our course was set to carry us up the center of the Straits between Kodiak and the Alaska Peninsula. As a result, we were hitting the wind and the waves head-on.

After a while it became necessary to hold on to the seats to keep from being tossed around inside the jeep like rocks in a tin can. We weren't making very good time, either, and Carlin finally decided to alter our course slightly so we would hit the waves at an angle and eventually bring us up to the south-western tip of the island.

Changing our course helped some, but it was still like riding a roller coaster that went from hump to drop with monotonous regularity hour after hour. Some time around three o ' clock

Carlin commented that we weren't much better off than we had been.

"What say we go back on course and make for the Straits again?" he said. "There' s a small cove just around the tip of the island. We can hole up there until this passes."

"All right with me," I answered. I much preferred to suffer the discomfort of a few hours of rough sea to going a day or more out of our way. I was getting anxious to end the ordeal.

So we changed from a roller coaster on nice smooth rails to one which seemed to prefer leapfrogging ditches. Time after time, after a wave had lifted us up some fifteen feet and then dropped us with a loud, bone-jarring crash, I was sure the jeep would split open and keep on going to the bottom.

Once I had to go top-side to use our open-air toilet. To prevent myself from being thrown off the jeep as well as to keep it from leaving me temporarily suspended in air, I had to cling to it like a leach. Every time a wave left us hanging in the air, I got in several seconds of astronaut-type training in weight-lessness.

Kodiak & the Deserted Cove

It was about eight o'clock in the evening and almost pitch-black because of a thick overcast by the time we began rounding the bulge of Kodiak' s northwestern hump. I had seen the cove on Carlin' s chart and it looked like its mouth was only a few hundred feet beyond the hump.

But because we were going against the wind, it was nearly two hours before Carlin gave me the signal to alter our course shoreward. All this time he had been standing in the hatchway, guiding us by the black blob of the coast-line faintly silhouetted against a murky sky.

Once we began turning I sighed with relief, expecting we would be tying up safe and sound within minutes. Peering out from my low window, it looked like we had only a few hundred yards to go. But we kept on going and going, and all I could see in any direction was velvety blackness.

I kept thinking the cove must be miles long, and wondering why Carlin didn't just direct us over to one side. Finally, after what seemed like hours, he ducked into the cabin.

"Shut her down!" he said.

I cut the engine, and after Carlin had moved back out of the hatchway, stuck my head up for a look. We were in a pit of Stygian darkness. I could see absolutely nothing except when I looked up at a sharp angle. Then I could make out the barest suggestion of a skyline.

I tossed the anchor out. We ate and then bedded down for the rest of the night—Carlin in the bunk and me hunched across the seats.

When I started waking up the next morning I had the feeling I was practically standing on my head. When I had regained enough of my senses to remember where I was, I found I was almost standing on my head.

The jeep was tilted over on one side, and from my position seemed ready to topple over any moment. My stirring woke Carlin. We both scrambled out of the hatch to see what was going on. We were almost on dry ground. The tide had gone out leaving one side of the jeep in a hole, which accounted for the crazy list.

My eyes swept the cove. It was beautiful. It was hemmed in on the east and west by steep hills. A fresh-water stream emptied into it from a grass-covered valley running southward.

The wide beach was clean white sand. A hundred and fifty feet or so up from the water's edge was a thick belt of bleached driftwood similar to the one we had seen on Makanru-to in the Kuriles.

To our right, overlooking the cove from a perch at the foot of the hill, was a small, sturdy-looking cabin.

There were several large wooden buildings—obviously abandoned—overlooking the spot where the fresh-water stream flowed into the bay. Inside the protected inlet, the water was perfectly calm and there was a warm sun shining. Looking back through the throat of the cove, I could see the waters of the strait were white and wild. The wind tunnel was still turned on and going full blast.

After climbing down off the jeep and looking about a bit, we found it was not quite as high and dry as we had first believed. A little pushing and rocking got it back on an even keel. Then we upped anchor and charged for the beach.

We hit a few small rocks going in, but the collisions were not solid enough to deflect the jeep off course, and we were soon on hard-packed sand.

With the tide out, there was a belt of wet sand some fifty feet wide, then a ring of white, loose sand with a hard crust just an inch or so down. We couldn't have asked for a better beach, and this time Carlin took no chances. He drove right up to the drift-wood obi before stopping.

We ate a leisurely breakfast then began exploring. We first checked out the cabin. It had two rooms with some furniture, including two bunks. A number of newspapers and magazines on a table were less than a year old, indicating the cabin had been occupied until the previous fall.

On the porch outside, I found a pair or rubber zori (sandals) and decided to take them for running around on the beach later. I scribbled a note, giving my name and address, and left it on the kitchen table. Some time after we left the cabin, Carlin noticed the zori in my hand.

"Where did you get those?" he asked

"Back at the cabin."

"What are you going to do with them?"

"Wear them."

He started getting excited. "They belong to somebody! That's stealing, you know!" he said harshly.

I was surprised at the vehemence of his words and wondered why he was taking it so seriously.

"I left a note saying I was borrowing them," I said. "But I don't think it makes much difference. They were outside of the cabin in the sun and would have rotted in a few months anyway."

Carlin wasn't interested in my reasoning, and mumbled something to the effect that if I wanted to take someone else's property to go ahead, he wouldn't be responsible.

From the cabin we retraced out steps to the jeep, then went on around the curving beach to where it was bisected by the stream. At the spot where the creek entered the sea, it was about two hundred feet across and had apparently once been deep enough to allow the passage of fairly large boats. Now most of the mouth was blocked by sand bars.

The buildings turned out to be an abandoned cannery and workers' quarters. Standing on the unloading dock overlooking the area where ships once anchored, we saw several hundred large salmon suspended motionless in the water. They looked so sluggish I thought we might catch one of them by hand.

The stream got shallow and narrowed to around thirty feet across only fifty yards up from the old cannery. I made my way along the high bank of the stream until I came to a place where I could climb down. Then I crossed the stream and approached the deep pool from the opposite side.

The fish weren't as lethargic as they looked. When I approached them they darted away. Salmon in the pool was a sign there would be some further along up the stream, where they would be more accessible. Anticipating some interesting camera shots, Carlin returned to the jeep and picked up his 16mm Bolex.

While he was gone, I took my trousers off and again tried to catch one of the fish in the pool, but they still had the advantage and I soon gave up the idea.

When Carlin got back we started up the stream. At the first shallow pool there were a few fish, but nothing worth filming. At the next pool, which was a little shallower, there were a few more fish. Two pools later the water was only six to ten inches deep, and the fish were so thick I could hardly take a step without pushing one aside to make room for my feet.

I picked up a stout stick and began driving the fish forward like a shepherd escorting a flock of sheep. There were silverbacks and humpbacks, and all of them were about two feet long.

Because of the shallowness of the pool, the humps of the fish were often out of the water. Out on the bank with his camera, Carlin got several seconds of the scene. After Carlin had all the film he wanted, we continued on up stream out of curiosity.

When we began to find fresh evidence of bears (the carcasses of fish out on the bank with only the entrails missing) we decided it was time to go back. We had no desire at all to meet an eight-feet tall Kodiak bear—especially one that might have young.

We had heard that when aroused, the bears could run up to forty miles an hour for short distances. Both Carlin and myself conceded we could not approach that speed, and chose to be discreet.

By the time we got back to Half-Safe it was afternoon. We had lunch and laid around on the sand for a couple of hours; safe and comfortable in our own private little cove. There was no question of getting underway. We could hear and see the wind howling down Shellikof Straits, churning the water into a white froth.

About mid-afternoon, Carlin announced he was going back up the stream to catch a fish for our supper. I got up to go along. As we started walking toward the old cannery, we noticed what looked like a small herd of cattle on the opposite side of the stream from us. When we got to the cannery we could see it was not cattle, but elk.

I decided to stay at the cannery, sit in the sun and watch the elk herd. Carlin searched the area until he found a sharp stick about four feet long and an inch in diameter, then he removed his shoes and took off, wading along the edge of the stream.

I picked a sunny place behind one of the buildings (all of which were built on pilings more than a dozen feet above ground as protection against high storm tides), removed my shirt and laid down.

Some two hours later I began to think something might have happened to Carlin, and started out to look for him. I had not taken more than ten steps when I saw him coming, slow-footed, down alongside the stream about a quarter of a mile away.

His bare feet had apparently got so tender from walking over gravel and rocks that he could hardly make any headway at all except when he found a patch of sand or mud. He sat down and rested his feet every twenty yards or so.

When he was about three hundred yards away, I saw he still had the stick he set out with, and impaled on it was a large fish. It turned out to be a humpback and a little under two feet long. He had speared it through the hump on the first thrust.

Back at camp we found a large tin can that had once had something like tomatoes in it, rigged a wire handle on it, scoured it out with sand, then filled it with fresh water from the jeep's tank.

While Carlin cleaned the fish, I collected firewood from the large supply at hand and soon had a blaze going. Half an hour later, Carlin judged the fish had been in the can long enough. We each helped ourselves to a large chunk. Except that it had somehow got sand in it, my piece was delicious, and I ate a second one.

By the time we had finished eating it was getting dark. In order to provide some light, I built up the cooking fire into a real campfire. We stretched out on the still warm sand and relaxed in comfort, occasionally gazing out across the cove to the sea beyond.

After the sun had been down for about half an hour, we saw a tiny pinpoint of light out on the Strait. As we watched, the light grew larger and larger. It soon became obvious it was a boat of some kind, heading for the cove. In about fifteen minutes the light was well inside the cove and we could hear the powerful roar of a big marine engine.

A short while later we could distinguish the dim outline of the boat as it approached the beach where we were camped. It was a cabin-cruiser that looked like it might sleep six to eight people. The boat pulled up to within a few hundred feet of the beach and stopped.

A man left the cabin, tossed out an anchor, then launched a small rowboat from the back of the cruiser. With swift strokes he rowed himself to the beach.

Carlin and I got up and were waiting for him at the water's edge. After jumping out of the rowboat, the man pulled it several feet up on the sand then turned to us. He was a tall, gaunt-faced man of about forty-five, wearing boots and woodsman's clothes. His stubble-bearded face was split by a wide grin. "I saw your fire from the straits. It was too rough to make any headway so I decided to come in."

While he was talking, his eyes took in our long beards and the jeep. His expression suddenly turned from friendly interest to surprised disbelief.

"Say! Are you that Ben Carlin fellow that's going around the world in a jeep?" he asked.

Carlin allowed that he was in a special, affected tone he regularly used to ridicule anyone who couldn't express himself well or asked a question he though was unnecessary.

The man was shocked into silence. He stared at Carlin in bewilderment. Then he recovered and began making admiring comments about the feat we had accomplished in coming all the way from Japan.

Whether these sincere remarks moved Carlin, or he had a change of heart for some other reason, he began responding to our visitor normally. We invited him to help himself to the salmon remaining in the can.

Known as "Slim," our visitor had been in Alaska and the Aleutians for over thirty years, and fancied himself a genuine sourdough. He had fished, hunted and prospected for gold throughout the islands. And he was a loner, doing most of this by himself. This impressed Carlin.

The man told us he had just finished working for a construction gang building an Army installation on the mainland side of the Straits opposite the cove. He had been using his yacht as a tugboat, helping unload supplies at an improvised harbor near the construction site. He had been headed toward the city of Kodiak on the southeastern end of the island when he spotted our fire.

"I cut straight across the channel hoping to find it a little smoother on this side, but it's rough all over," he explained.

The man's speech wasn't always grammatically correct, but he was an interesting story teller. We listened to him talk about the "old days" in Alaska for around two hours. Then he invited us to join him on his boat for the night.

"I got six good bunks, a gas stove and all the other comforts of home," he said.

After putting out our fire, we rowed to his boat and climbed aboard. Slim made coffee for us, and a short while later we went to bed. That night the wind whistling down the Strait got stronger and made itself felt in the cove. A few times I thought Slim's anchor had slipped and set us adrift.

The next morning the wind had subsided enough inside the cove that we didn't have to concern ourselves with it, but it was still murderous outside. Carlin and our host spent the morning talking. I read a book. About noon Slim baited a hook and threw it overboard.

"Should be able to come up with a chicken flounder before too long," he said.

Sure enough, about ten minutes later his line began to jerk. He pulled it in and with it came the first chicken flounder I'd ever seen. It looked like a thick kite with flappable wings.

After it was fried, I understood why it was known as chicken flounder. The flesh of the wings was tender, boneless and tasted so much like chicken steak it would have been difficult to tell the difference.

That afternoon, the cove began to take on the looks of a busy harbor. A large tug boat, pulling several barges, which we had been watching as it tried to buck the winds out in the Strait, gave up, pulled into the cove and anchored several hundred yards from us.

Slim started his boat and pulled up alongside the tug. An officer invited us aboard. By this time, grey clouds had blotted out the sun, and winds scooping down into the cove had turned cold. We were glad to go aboard the steam-heated tug, and spent the rest of the day sitting around, drinking coffee, talking and reading. That evening we ate in the tug's mess hall then returned to Slim's boat for the night.

The next morning the wind had died down considerably, and it appeared likely that it would quiet down more by that afternoon. Slim rowed Carlin and I back to the beach. We boarded Half-Safe and nosed out into the cove, dropping our anchor near Slim's cruiser and mooring our bow to his fantail.

Around noon Slim decided the weather had calmed down enough for him to chance the Strait again. Carlin and I got ready to cut loose from him, but the engine of his cruiser wouldn't start. A short had drained the batteries during the previous night.

We attached a cable to one of the jeep' s batteries and hooked it up to the cruiser. Just about the time we got the line from Half-Safe connected to the yacht' s battery, a Coast Guard patrol plane suddenly appeared and began making passes over us. The plane dropped a message saying they had been searching for the Half-Safe and wanted to know if Slim needed any help in rescuing us.

This made Carlin mad. It seemed that for years he had been fighting off people who wanted to rescue the ungainly looking contraption that was the Half-Safe—even when it didn't need it—and that was probably the sorest of his many sore points.

Carlin refused to let Slim answer the Coast Guard signal until he agreed to send exactly what Carlin told him to send. I forget the exact wording of the message Carlin wrote out for Slim, but in effect it told the Coast Guard that he wasn't rescuing the Half-Safe. The Half-Safe was rescuing him!

As soon as the battery hook-up was completed and Slim hit the starter button, the cruiser's engine started easily, but Slim was reluctant to take off with dead batteries and didn't want to set there in the cove for several hours racing his engine to charge them up.

He explained the situation to the master of the tug boat, who agreed to hook him up to the tug's giant generator. About two hours later his batteries were fully charged and he left the cove.

Shortly afterward, the tug and its covey of barges followed. We were again alone in the cove, and now it seemed a lonely, forsaken place.

Dolphins in the Night

Late that afternoon it was our turn. We headed out into the channel. By that time there were only a few white caps, but it took me a couple of hours to recondition myself to even that. The layover in the cove had spoiled me.

All that night and well into the next afternoon, we sped up the Straits at our usual fast clip of some two miles an hour. The weather was clear and with the coming of dawn we were treated — from a distance—to some of the most spectacular scenery in the world: the Valley of Ten Thousand Smokes.

A tremendous wilderness covering thousands of square miles on the Alaskan Peninsula, the Valley of Ten Thousand Smokes got its name from its dozens of active volcanoes. The volcanoes seldom belch lava, but they smoke continuously—hence the name.

From our position on the far side of Shellikof Straits, the valley, pock-marked by smoking cones, could have been the surface of some strange planet.

Late in the afternoon of that day, we arrived at the Williams' Cannery, located in a tiny inlet on the northeastern coast of Kodiak. The cannery was in operation, and ships were unloading when we pulled in. We tied up at the dock, and spent about an hour ashore.

We were in no hurry because we had to wait out the tide somewhere before attempting to make our next stop: Homer, on the tip of the Kenai Peninsula. About ten o'clock that night during one of my stints at the tiller, Carlin stood up in our lookout position, apparently attracted by the unusual beauty of the sea.

The sun was down just a far as it was going, and its soft rays had suffused the sky a pale pink. Then the pink overcast was broken here and there by dark brown and reddish clouds, which were puffy and loose. In contrast, the sea was blue-black and flat. A few minutes later Carlin ducked back into the cabin.

"Take a look outside," he said, motioning for me to let him take the tiller.

I took his place in the hatchway. We had been picked up by several porpoises which were putting on the most spectacular performance I had ever seen at sea. Like porpoises everywhere, these would alternately circle the jeep, dive under us from one side to the other, and then position themselves in front of Half-Safe and lead us for minutes at a time.

What made this particular occasion memorable was that the sea around us was fantastically phosphorescent. As the swift-moving dolphins cavorted in the black water, they appeared like comets leaving a glittering, golden trail behind them. We took turns watching this stellar display for nearly an hour, then the dolphins peeled off and left us.

I was reminded of what it might be like in deep space to briefly meet other travelers and then have them speed away on shining tails of light.

I Avoid a Collision

Some three hours later, or a little after two in the morning, Carlin was in the bunk asleep. The sea was flat, and as a result our horizon extended for a mile or more. I gradually became aware of a glow of light on the horizon in front of us, and after a few minutes, judged that it was moving in our direction. It was getting larger much faster than what our speed alone would have accounted for.

It looked to me like the running light of a ship. As it got closer and closer to us I began to be concerned that we might be run down. After all, from the wheel-house of a large ship running at full speed at night we would probably look like a dark blob on the surface of the sea—if anyone happened to notice us in the first place.

I changed course a few degrees to take us what I estimated would be two or three hundred yards to the left of the light. But the light kept getting bigger and moving faster, and was still bearing directly toward us despite our new course. Now very much concerned, I swung the jeep twenty degrees further left, and began wondering if I shouldn't wake Carlin.

The light loomed larger and closer. It appeared to be less than five hundred feet from us and coming in on a collision course. The skin on the back of my neck began to crawl and I felt like a flock of butterflies in my stomach had all become airborne at the same time.

Just when I was getting ready to hit the panic button, the light suddenly lifted off the surface of the water and magically became a round golden ball. It was the moon!

I had been trying to avoid a collision with the moon! I swung Half-Safe back on course and grinned sheepishly for the next half an hour.

"Boy!" I said to myself, "It was a good thing you didn't wake Carlin!"

The next morning we were treated to a second, even more magnificent view of the Valley of Ten Thousand Smokes.

The Sunning Seals

Around noon we reached a point between Shellikof Strait and Cook Inlet where the speed of the ebbing tide began to cancel out our own progress. Carlin gave the order to heave to and drop anchor. By this time the character of the water had changed until it no longer appeared like open ocean. There were no swells or waves, but the water was not still. It was flowing like a river, silent but swift.

As soon as the anchor hit bottom and caught, the line snapped tight from the drag of the jeep. We took a nap. Some three and a half hours later we awoke and found the sea around us stranger still. The water was no longer moving. It was dead calm. There was driftwood all about us, rocking gently in a faint breeze. And as far as we could see, great broad leaves of winged kelp striped the ocean. We were in a miniature Sargasso Sea.

Then, only a few feet from the jeep, we discovered a number of baby seals on kelp leaves sunning themselves. The little creatures were only about eight inches long and as thick as a man's forearm. They were aware of our presence and looked up at us with big sparkling eyes, unafraid.

Carlin got out his movie camera to photograph them. His movements and the noise of the camera disturbed some of them. They slid off their leafy perches into the water and disappeared. The others only sniffed at us. A few minutes later some adult seals came up and began playing around the jeep. After a while they lost interest in us and began moving away.

A short while later the tide was at its lowest, and we started up, intending to ride it all the way to Homer. We made excellent time, but were still three miles short of Homer when the tide reversed itself and began pouring out of Cook Inlet like someone had pulled the bung.

We had no choice but to sit it out again. By this time the Inlet had narrowed considerably. We were skirting the end of a small peninsula forming the southern side of Homer Bay, and pulled in to shore. There was deep water right up to a vertical three-foot bank. Knowing it would be dangerous to tie up too close to this bank, we moved out about fifty feet and tossed out the anchor. Then we went to sleep.

When we woke up the jeep was setting at a sharp angle. Just as it had in the cove at Kodiak, the receding tide had left us on an uneven keel. This time instead of a wheel in a hole, the nose of the jeep and one wheel were snagged on two rocks now breaking the surface of the water. The rest of Half-Safe was still floating.

There was a flurry of worried excitement until we determined that the continual rubbing of the jeep against the rocks had not caused any damage. There was some more apprehension for the safety of the jeep when we used the boat hook to pry ourselves off the rocks. But again there was no apparent damage.

It was then about five o'clock in the morning, and broad daylight. We had unknowingly anchored within a few hundred feet of three homes setting close to the water's edge. The noise we made getting underway disturbed a dog at one of the houses, and it came running down to the embankment, barking ferociously.

On Homer's Spit

We hit more rocks getting out into deeper water but the brunt of each impact was taken on the empty gas tank forming the jeep's prow, and no harm was done. A few minutes later we rounded the tip of the peninsula. About a mile and a half across a narrow-necked inlet was Homer.

To our right we could see a giant glacier filling a valley opposite Homer on our side of the inlet. It took us about half an hour to cross the neck of the inlet, circle a number of piers and come up to an area reserved for smaller boats.

There were boats all about, and a few lights gleaming faintly in the morning sun, but everything was quiet. Just about the time we finished getting the anchor out and mooring the jeep to the dock, a young man came out on the deck of a sixty-foot fishing boat about twenty-five yards away from us. The noise of the jeep's engine had apparently awakened him. He was rubbing sleep out of his eyes and yawning.

"How about a cup of coffee?" Carlin yelled to him.

"Huh?" he grunted.

Carlin repeated the question. By this time the young man was fully awake. He grinned hugely.

"Sure! Come on aboard!" he shouted. Then quickly stuck his head into a cabin porthole and began yelling, "Hey Jack! Get up! They're here! It's the Half-Safe guys!"

He repeated this several times, finally accompanying his yells with some vigorous banging on the side of the cabin. For some reason, he was really anxious to get Jack up. Carlin and I finished tying our shoes, climbed off the jeep onto the dock and started up the gangplank of the fishing boat.

We could hear the young man in the cabin still yelling for Jack to get up. When we reached the cabin lounge we discovered the reason for his anxiety. There was a girl lying on the couch, still asleep. She was a native girl in her twenties, dressed in a sweater and a pair of blue-jeans that had apparently been pulled on while she was lying down. Her panties were dangling from the ankle of one leg.

The young man was trying to arouse the girl when we walked in. He blushed furiously. The girl began coming out of her stupor. As soon as she came to, she grinned a rather sick grin, took her panties the rest of the way off, crumpled them in her hand and stuffed them into her back pocket. The young man then hustled her out of the lounge.

Moments later, Jack, who was apparently master of the ship, stuck his head out of his stateroom and mumbled a confused greeting. Looking back into his cabin uncertainly, he came out and shook hands with us. A moment later, a girl peeked out of his cabin, then lowered her head and scampered through the lounge.

Jack looked very embarrassed, gestured helplessly with his hands, and began talking about the welcome that had been planned for us by one of his friends. For the next two hours we were regaled by stories of what would have been in store of us if our arrival time had been known in advance.

The captain's friend owned and operated a "duck"—an amphibious vehicle similar to Half-Safe, but about four or five times larger. He had intended to come out to the mouth of Cook Inlet and escort us in. A reception committee was to have been waiting for us when we got there.

The captain was a very intense, earnest man and I regretted disappointing his friend. Carlin assured the captain that his reception, although not really prepared for us, was far more interesting than the official type. The captain winced and smiled weakly.

By mid-morning news of our arrival had spread through the community, and some two hundred people gathered at the harbor to see us, the jeep, and to marvel at the audacity of anyone who would attempt to cross the ocean in a contraption like Half-Safe.

Some of them appeared to doubt that it had actually been done. Others assumed that we had gone from one island to another as directly as possible and drove overland whenever there was land available—blissfully ignoring the fact that this would have been impossible for many elementary reasons.

When noon-time approached, we were invited by a restaurant owner to be his guests for lunch. Several carloads of people followed us from the harbor to the restaurant. Our host asked us if we would mind signing autographs for the children. When we assented, a line dozens of kids long formed immediately, running from outside the restaurant in through the dining room to our table.

When I signed for the host's young son and daughter, he noted my Phoenix, Arizona address. It turned out that my parents lived next door to his sister-in-law who at that moment was in Anchorage. He insisted I stop in to see her when we arrived in that city.

Late that afternoon, the captain's friend, who had been out of town, showed up and arranged and impromptu party for us that evening at his home. Several of the town's more prominent citizens attended the party, and it was a fine party as parties go.

The captain's friend was enthusiastic and sincere. As could be expected, he rubbed Carlin the wrong way.

Several times during the evening Carlin cut him to the quick by some patently sarcastic response that quick-froze the atomsphere for a number of minutes and left everyone embarrassed and fidgety. About the fifth or sixth time this happened, I managed to get the man aside and "explain" Carlin's behavior.

I told him Carlin was an eccentric even for an Australian who had worked in China and served in the Indian Army. I don't think he fully understood the explanation but he began to counter Carlin's poisoned barbs with gusto. The party might have ended in a sordid brawl except for the fact that the man's wife was a beautiful, gracious, lady, and Carlin apparently felt obliged to restrain himself.

That night we were lodged as guests of the town's leading motel . The following day we were invited to be the guests of honor at a luncheon staged by the town council. It was a formal affair with some fifty people in attendance, including the local news correspondent.

After we had eaten and some opening remarks had been made by the leaders of the council, Carlin and I were asked to respond. I was nominated to speak first. I knew very well how Carlin would react if I began to recount some of our adventures in detail, so I was brief. I thanked the council for the invitation to address them but declined.

"It is Carlin's story, and I think he should be the one to tell it," I said.

That required less than five seconds, and there was a little round of applause when I sat down. Carlin stood up and paused, looking at the audience. I had never heard him speak formally and was looking forward to it. When he wanted to be, he was a witty, entertaining conversationalist, and no doubt a polished speaker.

Carlin noticed the news correspondent seated near the center of the long table was busily scribbling notes on memo paper. Addressing himself to the group, Carlin said in so many words:

"I would like to request that absolutely no notes be taken of what I am about to say. This story is my 'bread and butter' and I want to be the one to profit from it. I'm sure you can understand that."

There was an outbreak of creaking chairs as everyone attempted to locate the offending newsman, and a number of murmured approvals of Carlin's request. The reporter wadded up the page of notes he had taken, stuffed them into a coat pocket and leaned back in his chair, a slightly embarrassed look on his face.

Carlin began. He had not spoken more than ten words when he suddenly stopped, red in the face and eyes blazing. The reporter had picked up his pencil and was scratching on his note-pad.

"There'll be no speech as long as that nincompoop remains in the room!" Carlin said in a loud, angry voice. At the same time he sat down.

There was shocked silence. Again everyone in the room turned their eyes toward the news correspondent. He flushed red. The silence continued. It gradually became apparent that the man wasn't going to leave on his own volition and that none of his friends or neighbors was going to tell him to leave.

A low murmur rose among a few of the people at the far end of the table who were evidently not close friends of the reporter. Their words were not clearly audible but they were obviously making disparaging remarks about the newsman's behavior.

The babble gained in volume, and soon people all around the table were doing their best to salvage the tenor of the meeting. Someone stood up. Others followed, and gradually people formed little groups, all talking in subdued but determined voices. Then by twos and threes they began to leave the room. The two persons who had been acting as our guides spent several minutes making oblique apologies to Carlin and trying to talk away their embarrassment.

The food I had eaten felt like it had soured.

Breaching Cook Inlet

A short while later one of our hosts took us on a tour of the area by car then returned us to the harbor where we spent the remainder of the afternoon sitting around and talking to others—not to each other.

Our departure was set for early that evening just before the tide was due to start up the inlet. A large crowd gathered to see us off. Our host of the night before launched his duck with a party of friends aboard, and began cruising around in the outer harbor waiting for us.

There was no lack of good humor and noise—among people who had not been at the luncheon—as we rumbled out of the harbor and headed toward the end of the spit separating the harbor from Cook Inlet. It was the best send-off we had had since leaving Wakkanai.

The faster, much larger "duck" accompanied us for a mile or so, capering around like a speed boat compared to our slow, majestic pace. After we waved farewell to the people on the duck and were well out of sight of the harbor, Carlin called a halt. Always thorough, he wanted to lengthen our anchor line for the layover he knew would have to made en route up the inlet to Anchorage.

The line was already about one hundred feet long. We added another hundred and fifty feet-not because the inlet was so deep, but because the flatter the anchor line could lay in relation to the bottom, the greater its holding power. We would need every ounce of holding power we could get when the tide started pouring out of the inlet at speeds of more than ten miles an hour.

After splicing the line, we got underway again just about dusk. The water was still, then; the calm before the inrush began. We quickly steamed out to the center of the inlet to catch the full force of the swelling tide.

For the next eight hours we fairly whizzed along, the speed of the tide added to our own. Then sometime after midnight, Carlin announced it was time to anchor and brace ourselves for the coming onslaught. At that point, the stampeding waters deserting the upper reaches of the long inlet sometimes attained speeds of fifteen miles an hour.

Carlin had waited until the last minute to stop. As soon as the engine was cut we started drifting backwards. I tossed the anchor overboard. Seconds after the last of the line had jumped out of my hand, the drift of the jeep took up the slack. We could feel the anchor being dragged along the bottom, the flukes grasping for a hold. Then one of them found the bottom and dug in. The Half-Safe shuddered to a stop.

But just when we started to relax, the anchor slipped and we drifted several more yards before it caught again. This time its grip on the bottom seemed solid.

We waited for half an hour to see if the anchor was going to hold. When it did, we decided to take a chance and try to get some sleep.

When we awoke at dawn it didn't take much seamanship to tell we were drifting. The anchor had lost its hold and was being dragged along the bottom. I pulled it in as rapidly as possible to see what had happened.

When it broke the surface, caked with mud, it hardly looked like an anchor any more. One of the steel flukes had been bent over almost parallel with the shaft. This was surprising enough but it was even more surprising that the fluke had bent rather than the line parting.

From the shoreline visible on our right, Carlin judged we had drifted more than twenty miles back down the inlet. Without an anchor there was no question of trying again to breach the rampaging waters.

We were then drifting sideways at somewhere around seven miles an hour. Carlin elected to make for Kenai, a small settlement on a bluff overlooking a side-arm of Cook Inlet, about fifteen miles southeast of where we were at that moment.

He started the jeep up and swung us around so we were running with the current. Half-Safe seemed to have sprouted wings.

The Last of the Sea

Over the next hour we gradually angled away from the main channel of the inlet toward the side-arm leading to Kenai. Carlin estimated it was about a four-hour run. He gave me a heading, then climbed into the bunk and went to sleep.

Two hours later I woke him. He stood up in the hatchway to relieve himself and look around. Seconds later he was back in the cabin, fuming and grabbing for the tiller.

When he had given me the compass heading before going to sleep, I assumed it was to be our course until I roused him two hours later. He had either misjudged the distance we would cover in two hours or had simply forgotten to give me a change of course effective some time before he got up.

It wasn't the first time this had happened. Compared with past demonstrations, however, this outburst was tame. For the next hour he stood in the hatch giving me frequent course changes, gradually working us up alongside the bluff on which Kenai set.

Someone had spotted us when we were still more than an hour out, and most of the settlement of some one hundred people were on the bluff watching when we pulled in.

There were a number of small boats tied up behind a makeshift breakwater just beneath the bluff, and Carlin made for this area.

When we got behind the breakwater we could see where the bluff gave away to a fairly gradual slope at the far end of the tiny man-made harbor. We headed in that direction. As soon as the people on the bluff saw where we were going, they rushed around to the slope and came down to the water.

The slope wasn't so steep a vehicle couldn't get up it under its own power, but it had rained recently and the blue-grey mud making up the lower half was obviously slick as ice.

Again the townspeople knew about us and it took only a few seconds to get across the idea we would need help in getting

Half-Safe out of the water and up the slope to level ground. Several of the men responded instantly.

A moment later a truck had been backed down on the slope to where the mud began. In the meantime, I was on the prow with my tow line at the ready. When we were about ten feet from shore, I jumped in, carrying the line with me.

Someone on shore took it and ran it to the back of the truck where it was quickly made fast. Then with half a dozen people acting as coordinators, Carlin and the truck driver tried to engage their wheels at the same time.

On the first attempt the truck's wheels began spinning as soon as the jeep came up against the lip of the shoreline. Almost immediately several dozen men and boys ranged themselves along the tow rope, and at a given signal, all pulled. This made the necessary difference. Half-Safe left the water for what was to be the last time and was unceremoniously hauled up the slippery slope by its nose.

During the few minutes it had taken us to get the jeep out of the water, the grey overcast sky had darkened and now it began to rain lightly. I stowed the bow tow and other lines that had been out on deck in one of the baskets on top of the jeep while Carlin got out tools to remove the rudder and propeller.

The rain began to thicken. Most of the crowed watching us retreated to their cars and trucks or the few buildings spotted along the bluff road. A few stayed on until we had the prop shaft and rudder off and stowed away.

One of the men who had been a leader in helping get the jeep out of the water invited us to join him and his wife in a nearby tavern for a celebration drink.

Afterward, when it was learned that the couple lived a few miles down the highway in the direction we were going, Carlin offered to give the man a ride in the jeep, leaving the man's wife to bring up the rear in their car.

For the first couple of miles, I sat outside on top of Half-Safe. When the rain started falling in earnest, I transferred to the car. That night the couple put us up in their guest cabin.

Anchorage and the End

Our next stop after leaving Kenai the following morning was a highway restaurant about an hour outside of Anchorage. It had taken us all that afternoon to drive up the Kenai Peninsula, and was then about eight o'clock in the evening. Our only meal that day had been the late breakfast served to us by our hosts of the night before.

My arrangement with Carlin was that while at sea I would eat from the jeep's store of food, but I was responsible for providing for myself while we were ashore. I had been waiting for him to stop for more than two hours so we could get something to eat.

I had just about resigned myself to waiting until we got to Anchorage when Carlin started pulling over at the restaurant.

"Let's get a cup of coffee," he said.

His action surprised me. But then I realized it was a shrewdly calculated move on Carlin's part, and had little or nothing to do with eating. He knew it would not be to our advantage to drive into Anchorage unannounced and at night. By stopping at a public place, the word was sure to spread like rumor and there would be time for people to prepare for us in whatever way caught their fancy.

When we started to climb down from Half-Safe I recalled that I didn't have any money in my pocket.

"My money is stowed away in my duffle bag. I don't have any on me," I said.

Carlin gave me a funny look. "I don't have any money!" he mimicked with a sneer. "Are you so cheap you expect other people to feed you?" he asked in a scornful tone of voice.

I had thought there was nothing more Carlin could say or do that would surprise me, but this caught me off balance. For someone who had spent several of the last ten years as a "professional" guest of so many hundreds of people around the world, his holier-than-thou, sarcastic attitude was the last thing I expected.

For what I hoped would surely be the last time, I resisted an almost overwhelming urge to crush his skull with the nearest blunt instrument.

"I'll wait until we get to Anchorage and unpack," I said, climbing back on the jeep.

Then he surprised me again. "Come on! I'll pay for it!" he said.

"I can wait," I replied.

Then for some reason still a mystery he became insistent that I accept the offer. I decided it would be silly to sit outside and wait for an hour or more, and went on in with him. I thought he intended to eat, and I was starving.

The restaurant was large and fairly plush. I was slightly ill-at-ease about walking into it in the same outfit I'd worn since leaving Japan, but my concern quickly disappeared. As soon as we stepped through the door a man at a nearby table called out to Carlin and invited us to join him. He was a Reeves Airways pilot Carlin had met on Cold Bay.

Extra chairs were pulled up and we joined the man, his lady companion and another couple. They had just finished eating and were having their coffee. The man asked us if we would like something to drink.

Both Carlin and I said coffee would be fine. When we left the restaurant some time later, coffee was all we had had, and I was hungrier than ever.

From the restaurant we drove on a short distance to an all-night filling station, where Carlin got an okay from the man in charge to park the jeep near the station for the night. Then with very poor grace, he offered me some food from the jeep's store.

Afterward we bedded down; myself in the jeep and as usual, Carlin outside on top of the cabin.

An hour or so after dawn the next morning we began stirring around. There was already some traffic along the street and the jeep began to attract attention. A number of people working in the vicinity of the gas station came up, wandered around the jeep a couple of times and stared at us curiously but silently.

After a while one young man came up while Carlin and I happened to be inside the jeep. Instead of standing back and circling us warily as the others had done, he walked right up to the side of the jeep and peered in at us.

Carlin called him a few names and told him to go away, but Carlin's voice apparently didn't carry through the cabin wall because the man didn't respond. He kept peering in and finally tried to engage us in conversation. Carlin exploded.

"Get away you stupid monkey!" he screamed.

The young man backed off, as if he had been slapped, and walked away quickly.

"That wasn't necessary," I said. "Driving around in a thing like this what do you expect people to do? Where would you be if they didn't pay any attention to you?"

Carlin turned on me. "Keep your fucking nose out of my business, you worthless shit ! You nothing!" he grated viciously. Looking at him, I had the impression he had just about driven himself to the breaking point.

Up to that moment, I had been undecided about whether or not to continue on with him after we arrived in Anchorage. This newest incident was the deciding factor. My obligation to him was to go as far as Anchorage, and we were practically there. I now resolved that as soon as the official welcome in Anchorage was over, I would shuck him and my dirty clothes at the same time.

Not only would I be done with him several months earlier, but that would also allow me to keep a promise I made to my family to get to Phoenix as quickly as possible to see my ailing mother.

A little while after this yelling incident, the owner of a restaurant in Anchorage drove up and presented us with guest cards good for any number of free meals at his place of business for as long as we were in the city.

Several other cars, including a police cruiser, had accompanied the restaurant owner out to where we had spent the night. When we climbed into the jeep for the last few miles to Anchorage, the police car led the way.

Our first stop in Anchorage was at the office of Reeves Aleutian Airways. There we met Mrs. Reeves and one of her daughters, and were interviewed by the press.

MAIL CALL—On our arrival in Anchorage I received a stack of letters from the mailman. The letters had been addressed to me c/o of Anchorage, Alaska, and held by the post office until Carlin and I showed up—exactly four months to the day after we left Tokyo, Japan. (Anchorage Times photo)

Afterward, the local public relations director for an oil company invited us to lunch, and there offered Carlin an interesting sum of money to park the Half-Safe alternately at the company's various service stations around the city. Carlin accepted the offer, and after we got our Alaska drivers' licenses we drove the jeep to the firm's leading station.

Soon afterward, the news of our arrival and the location of the jeep was being advertised on the radio every few minutes. In no time a crowd gathered at the station and put us through the usual third degree about the jeep. Every other person wanted to know what we did to keep from getting bored while at sea.

In the crowd that gathered around the jeep was an Australian woman who rented rooms in her home. She invited us to be her guests while we were in Anchorage. Her invitation was accepted immediately. Then began a round of lunches and dinners that lasted for the next two days.

Mid-morning of the third day, I happened to go back to our lodgings and learned from our host that Immigration officials had been trying to get in touch with Carlin and myself since our arrival. We were supposed to have checked in with them immediately. I went down and had my passport stamped, and managed to get the word to Carlin about noon.

That afternoon I was asked by a third person while in Carlin's presence if I intended to stay with the Half-Safe all the way to Montreal, where the jeep had officially started the trip some seven years before.

I answered that I intended to resign from the enterprise as soon as I wasn't needed to fulfill the agreement Carlin had made with the local oil company. While I was talking, Carlin glared at me disdainfully. When I finished he rapped out belligerently:

"Don't stay on my account!"

"All right," I said. "I'll leave as soon as I can get air reservations."

A short while later, I left Carlin and booked passage on North-west Airlines leaving Anchorage at seven the next morning.

I was not to see Carlin again. That evening I went out to dinner with a university classmate who happened to be in Anchorage at the time. After dinner I joined another group for a party that lasted all night.

At five o'clock in the morning my party hosts drove me to where Carlin and I were staying.

An airport limousine was to pick me up there at five fifteen. My duffle bag was already packed. I went into the house for it then returned to the sidewalk outside to wait for the car.

I had heard Carlin snoring in his room, but there was no one up. I was careful not to make any noise. A few minutes later our benefactress came out in her housecoat. She must have heard me come in.

"You're leaving," she stated matter-of-factly.

"Yes, I am," I replied.

"I don't blame you," she said. After a slight pause, she added: "I've met his kind before."

Then, as if the subject of my erstwhile partner was closed, she talked about her plans to return to Australia the following year. Her American husband had died a few months earlier and she was going back home to be with her relatives.

She gave me the address of her family in Australia, and invited me to drop in for a visit if I ever got that far south. Then the limousine came and I was on my way to the airport.

And so ended my association with Half-Safe and its acerbated master who was not really its master after all, but its slave.

It had not been a pleasant association; not even for a moment. The few hours of pleasure experienced during the trip always came from the outside.

Looking back on the trip, I do not think I proved myself courageous. Considering the circumstances and purpose of the hazardous adventure, I was more likely a candidate for a dunce's cap than anything else. Yet once it was done there was some satisfaction in having risked my life on an absurd undertaking, above and beyond the ego gratification I got from being singled out and fussed over.

I felt the trip had toughened me mentally. I knew it had been good for me physically. When I left Tokyo on May 3, I had just gotten over pneumonia and was more than ten pounds under weight. When we arrived in Anchorage four months later, I was ten pounds over my normal weight, and this extra poundage was made up of new muscles and calluses. My only physical complaint was soft, sore gums from not brushing my teeth regularly during the voyage.

Even though I could claim very little credit for the successful completion of the crossing—Carlin carried the burden and can have the glory—I was still able to say to myself, "It was a tough test in more than one way. But you passed. That is something!"

—END—

POSTSCRIPT

Some five years later, when visiting my parents in Phoenix, Arizona from Tokyo (to which I had returned shortly after ending the jeep trip), one of my sisters reported that Carlin had come through Phoenix, called my parent's home, and not finding me there invited them to a private showing of the film he had taken while we were on the voyage.

My sister said he was the epitome of courtesy and charm, and regaled them for several hours with stories about our adventure.

Another five years later, by which time I had spent another decade in Japan and the Orient and moved to Phoenix, Arizona where my family and my wife's family lived, I received a phone call from a friend who was aware of the jeep adventure.

He was very excited, and began asking me questions about Half-Safe—was it yellow, did it have commercial signs painted on it, was it covered like a tank, have a pennant hanging from a mast, and so on. I said yes to all of his questions.

"I just followed that damn thing through half of Phoenix!" He yelled.

I later learned that it had taken Carlin several months to drive the jeep down the Alcan Highway through Alaska and Canada to California, with a number of mishaps along the way, including driving it into a ditch while drunk.

He then drove across the country to New York, and finally up to Nova Scotia, where the successful Atlantic crossing had started in the late 1940s.

My friend spotting the Half-Safe in Phoenix some 10 years after our arrival in Anchorage, Alaska made it obvious that Carlin was still a slave to the jeep; that it had become is life.

#

Lightning Source UK Ltd.
Milton Keynes UK
UKOW031835020412

190034UK00003B/103/A